A Refreshing As Snow In The Hot Summertime

God Bless You

Joanne Wallace

Ps. 139

His Burden is Light

2003 - Women's Retreat

OUR SAVIOR LUTHERAN CHURCH

This devotional book is lovingly presented to you from the 2003 Women's Retreat Committee

Come to me all who are weary and burdened, and I will give you rest. Take my yoke upon you and learn from me, for I am gentle and humble in heart, and you will find rest for your souls. For my yoke is easy and my burden is light.

Matthew 11:28-30

As Refreshing As Snow In The Hot Summertime

Joanne Wallace
Deanna Wallace

Printed in the United States of America

ISBN: 1-880527-04-9

Dedication

To my beautiful grandchildren:

Robby, Aron, Kimmi,
Jameson, Shaina, Elijah,
Fallon and Tadela

--JW

To Donna Hartley,
who has always
brought unlimited love
and "snowy refreshment"
to our friendship.

--DW

Other Books by Joanne Wallace:

The Image of Loveliness
How To Be Your Best
Dress With Style
Dress To Fit Your Personality
The Confident Woman
The Working Woman
Starting Over Again
Mini-Memories For Image Bearers

Contents

Acknowledgments

From Joanne:

Thank you, Sherline Montgomery, for your wonderful editing skills on the final manuscript.

Thank you also to my dear husband, Robert, for your patience, encouragement, and excitement about the book.

A special thanks to my ten diligent prayer-partners who have prayed for this book and for my ministry to women. You are always such a great source of encouragement -- full of love and wisdom. I will be eternally grateful to the Lord for allowing you into my life as my close "forever" friends. God bless you for your unending love for God's ministry.

Carol Brockway
Judy Chase
Janice Gutierrez
Diane Hopper
Rita Lamphere
Becky Martin
Sherline Montgomery
Anne Regel
Laura Lou Tolles
Pat Voth

I also want to acknowledge my weekly Bible study group and the "50+" group of women from my church who have prayed for the outcome of this book.

From Deanna:

Thank you, BJ Plaster, for your wonderful support and invaluable help in taking care of my family while I have tried to work on this book. You are such a blessing to me!

Thank you also to my children: Robby, Aron, Kimmi, Jameson, Shaina, Elijah, Fallon, and Tadela for your understanding when mom was just "too busy."

My deep appreciation to Donna Hartley, Dan Cox, and Waruingi wa Mungai, for encouragement, love, and support while I tried desperately to finish this project.

Why This Book Was Written

This book is designed to be like refreshing snow in the middle of your swelteringly heated and busy life. It is designed to be a tool to help you pull away from your hurried schedule so that you can be regenerated. As you read each story, it is our prayer that your life will be revived and renewed, especially in your daily walk with the Lord.

The stories in this book are purposefully short and to the point. Who has time to waste? Each story is complete in itself and will hopefully provide a little "snow" in your hot summertime lifestyle. At one sitting you can read just one of the stories, or several, depending on the time you have available.

In this energetic and fast-paced world we can all use a little refreshment from the heat. So, in the words of the old winter song, "Let it snow! Let it snow! Let it snow!"

--JW & DW

On Bent Knees

There is a true story that has been told about the sculptor, Thorealdsen. After this important artist had completed his very famous statue of Christ, he invited a friend of his to come and see it. In Thorealdsen's statue, Christ's arms are extended, with His head hanging between His arms.

"I think your sculpture is beautiful," said Thorealdsen's friend, "but I cannot see Christ's face."

In answer, the great sculptor smiled gently, "If you would see the face of Christ," he said, "you must first get on your knees."

This little gem of a story is one of my favorites. It reminds me that my attitude toward Christ should be one of worship and humility. It is absolutely true that in order for me to really see Christ's face, I must first get on my knees.

Have you been on your knees lately? It is not the most glamorous place to be, but it sure does inspire a sense of reverence, humbleness, and awe – which is appropriate under the circumstances. After all, you are coming before the Most High God over the entire universe. If that does not make you bend your knees, nothing will!

"Come, kneel before the Lord our Maker."

Psalm 95:6

Wake Up!

I do *not* like to wake up. It is no problem for me to stay up late at night, but waking up in the morning is for the birds! It takes me at least an hour to become fully awake – sometimes even longer. Until a couple of years ago, I definitely could not wake up unless I had had my morning coffee. Recently I have given up the coffee, but not until I learned a valuable lesson.

One morning I sleepily walked down the stairs from my bedroom into the kitchen for my morning cup of coffee. My husband always had a fresh cup waiting for me because he knew I could not wake up without it. With my eyes half closed I reached for the waiting cup and sleepily made my way over to the table to sit down. Although I was still not awake, I began to sip my coffee. The first swallow was hot, just the way I liked it. The second swallow was good, but something seemed wrong. By the third swallow, I fuzzily wondered what I was missing. In my confused state I said, "This coffee tastes a little bit funny."

Looking up from his paper, my husband began to laugh. To my chagrin, he could not stop laughing as he replied, "Well, that is because I have not put any coffee in the cup yet! I was just pre-heating the cup with hot water!"

With his laughter jolting me, my sleepy eyes suddenly popped wide open and stared into my coffee cup. Sure enough, I was drinking plain hot water! If I had not been so blind I would have realized it much sooner.

I have now learned to open my eyes and check things out before I assume I am drinking the right mixture. Open eyes have some real advantages! The same holds true for spiritual sight. If you are looking for the adventure of a lifetime, ask God to open your eyes. His plan for you will take your breath away. If your life looks like plain hot water, why not allow God to put the coffee in your cup? It will make all the difference!

Some of us need to ask God to restore sight to our spiritually blind eyes. God has a special and wonderful plan for each one of us; He is just waiting to open our eyes so that we can begin to fulfill His plan. Christ will not stop you from leading your own life, but in kindness He asks, "Why? Do you know the future like I do? Why trust your blind eyes more than My far-seeing ones?" Remember that it brings great delight for God to restore sight to blind eyes. If you have been spiritually blind, having your eyes opened means you can now catch glimpses of His Power and overwhelming Love. It also means a new vision, a new world, a new you.

How can your eyes be opened? Through time spent reading God's Word and one-on-one meditation time with Christ. Just time spent with Him and the world is changed! Can you, with all your activity and busy work make the same claim? Spend more and more time in communion with Him and your eyes will be opened to a brand new life.

Christ loves you in spite of your sleepy, tired, or blind eyes. But, why not wake up and *see* the coffee? You might be missing something!

"Then Jesus told him, 'I have come into the world to give sight to those who are spiritually blind and to show those who think they see that they are blind."

John 9:39

Expecting The Unexpected

Suddenly the front door swung open and my husband charged through the door yelling, "That is it! I am going back to being a couch potato!" He ran for the kitchen and grabbed a glass of water, all the while spluttering and grumbling about something I could not quite catch.

I was utterly bewildered. Just that morning my husband had decided it was time to start riding his bicycle to work. Since it was only a fifteen-minute ride, he figured it would help him stay in shape, save gas money, and reduce wear and tear on his car. It was a beautiful, breezy, warm day in Northern California and he had left for work with a smile on his face; excited about his new adventure in transportation.

Now here he was, back home, looking and sounding like a wounded bear. As he continued to drink the cool water, I tried to find out what was wrong.

"Was the bike ride too exhausting for you?" I asked.

"No."

"Was the sun too hot?"

"No."

"Did your bike break down?"

"No. No. No. It is not my body giving out, the sun being too hot, or a problem with the bike."

"Well, what is it then?"

"You will not believe it! I was riding to work just fine, having a great time, when a bee flew into my mouth and stung me!"

He was right -- I could not believe it! Life had given my husband an unexpected whammy! Despite his best made plans for how this biking adventure would be accomplished, he never figured in a bee sting.

Have you ever had a similar experience? Well, maybe you have not had a bee fly into your mouth and sting you, but what about some other strange happening? Have you ever thought you had figured out all the angles so that things would turn out perfectly, only to discover something unexpected totally changed your plans?

It is a perplexing, but important lesson to realize that we cannot even know what will happen in the very next moment. We can take that knowledge with calm acceptance and trust, or we can wring our hands and fight against the circumstances. Either way, we have to face the reality of dealing with the unexpected. For many of us, this lesson is difficult to grasp. We want to control our days and have everything go according to plan. We do not want any unexpected "bee stings."

Clearly, God has a way of reminding us not to trust in our own plans. Things like bee stings point out our shortcomings in organizing the daily affairs of our lives. If we cannot even manage the simple day-to-day stuff, what makes us think we can manage the really important matters? I think it would be better to leave the planning to Someone with better insight!

In love, Christ reminds us that we need to trust Him in *everything*. Unless we surrender everything to Him, including all of our best made plans, we cannot fully appreciate all of the abundance in life that *He* has planned.

You can trust God for both the expected and the unexpected events in life. After all, the unexpected is only unexpected to you -- there is nothing unexpected to Him.

"We can make our plans, but the final outcome is in God's hands."

Proverbs 16:1.

"Since the Lord is directing our steps, why try to understand everything that happens along the way?"

Proverbs 20:24

Just One Race - The Human Race

It was 1961, and we were living in Seattle, Washington. My daughter, Deanna, was almost three years old. It was the time in our nation's history when the southern part of the United States still had separate drinking fountains for *whites* and *coloreds*. The Civil Rights Movement was just gaining national momentum.

One day I took Deanna to a park where other children were playing. I pushed her on the swing and merry-go-round and followed her as she toddled all over the place. It was not long before she became thirsty and headed for the drinking fountain with me following behind her. Before Deanna reached her goal, a little African-American girl skipped over to get a drink too. Deanna just stopped right in her tracks and stood very quiet and still. I came up right beside her and we both stood watching the little girl. Bending down, I whispered in Deanna's ear, "Isn't she beautiful?

Look at her pretty hair and brown skin. She looks different from you, but Deanna, remember this: we *are all the same on the inside.*"

Many times through the years Deanna has recounted this story to me. It is one of her earliest memories and one of the experiences that has deeply shaped her life. According to Deanna, my words permeated her. They sank all the way down into the deepest recesses of her heart and then spread throughout her entire body, mind, spirit, and belief system. Deanna was only a toddler, but she *heard* me. *We are all the same on the inside.* Those words have shaped her life.

It was not until years later that Deanna realized those words did not come naturally to me. They were not the words I heard as a child. I had grown up with racial prejudice as an acceptable part of life. I had made a conscious decision to change my daughter's outlook through my words. I did not want her to grow up with bigotry.

Did I know that my words would open the door to my little girl's heart? Could I have guessed that one day my daughter would open her heart and home to children from all over the world? Thank God that Deanna listened to His calling. She now has children with various cultural and ethnic backgrounds such as East Indian, Korean, Ethiopian, Native American, and African-American. My beautiful, adopted, international family of grandchildren is a living testimony to the truth of these words: We *are all the same on the inside.*

I am glad that I chose love over bigotry. It has not only changed my life, but the lives of many others. My grandchildren, with all their varying skin colors, are the greatest joy to me. As Deanna has often said to me, "There is only one race, the *human* race."

"He created all the people of the world from one man, Adam, and scattered the nations across the face of the earth..."

Acts 17:26

"Little children, let us stop just <u>saying</u> we love people; let us <u>really</u> love them, and <u>show it</u> by our <u>actions</u>."

I John 3:18

News Of My Death Has Been Greatly Exaggerated

    While vacationing in Maui, I called home to receive the messages left on my answering machine. I wanted to keep up on my business obligations even while on vacation. To my astonishment, I heard a very unexpected message from a woman who had great sadness in her voice. She said,

    "I have just heard the tragic news that Joanne Wallace is dead. Please call me and tell me if this is really true. I heard her speak years ago and I am very saddened by this news. My phone number is..."

    It was quite a shock to receive the news of my own death. Could it be true, I wondered? I mean, vacationing in Maui is close to earthly paradise, and some days I was enjoying myself so much I thought I must have passed on to glory. I pinched myself to make sure. Yes, I was most definitely still alive!

Immediately I dialed the woman's number so that I could reassure her. Unfortunately, in her grief, she had given me an incorrect number. (Have you ever remembered everyone else's phone number but not your own?) Since I could not reach this woman I did not have a clue as to how to squelch the rumor. What if the rumor spread and people stopped asking me to speak, assuming of course, that I would not be able to book the engagement from heaven?

I considered my possibilities. Maybe I should call up all my friends and say, "Hey, I am still alive. Just wanted to let you know. Please pass the word." Or I could send out official letters with various testimonials and doctor's opinions stating that on very good medical authority I was most certainly not dead. Better yet, I could take out an ad in a national newspaper with a large picture of myself captioned "She's Alive." Would that squelch the rumor? I doubt it. Hey, I am a realist. We live in a society where Elvis is still sighted at the local Burger King!

I felt powerless against this rumor. It made me realize how important it is to speak only the truth. Passing on rumors, innuendo, or gossip can cause such heartache for so many. The woman who called me was trying to do the right thing; she was calling to check out the facts, but what about the person who gave her the information in the first place?

We need to learn not to pass along gossip or information until we have gotten the true story. Even a small untruth, spoken out loud, can cause extensive damage in someone's life.

(By the way, if you are one of those people that heard the rumor about my death, maybe you can help me spread the word. So far I am still here alive and kicking!)

"Get the facts at any price, and hold on tightly to all the good sense you can get."

Proverbs 23:23

"Truth stands the test of time; lies are soon exposed."

Proverbs 12:19

Nobody's Friend

When I consider all the damage that can be done by gossip, I am reminded of the startling poem I once read in *Dear Abby's* column. Although the author of the poem is unknown, the words ought to be memorized by all of us.

My name is gossip.
I have no respect for justice.
I maim without killing.
I break hearts and ruin lives.
I am cunning and malicious and gather
strength with age.
The more I am quoted,
the more I am believed.

My victims are helpless.
They cannot protect themselves
against me because I have
no name and no face.
To track me down is impossible.

The harder you try,
the more elusive I become.
I am nobody's friend.

Once I tarnish a reputation,
it is never the same.
I topple governments
and wreck marriages.
I ruin careers and cause sleepless nights,
heartaches, and indigestion.
I make innocent people cry
in their pillows.
Even my name hisses.
I am called Gossip.
I make headlines and headaches.

Before you repeat a story,
ask yourself:
Is it true?
Is it harmless?
Is it necessary?
If it isn't, don't repeat it.

"Any story sounds true until
someone tells the other side
and sets the record straight."

Proverbs 18:17

Beauty In His Eyes

After a speaking engagement in an Oregon coastal town a few years ago, I received the most heartwarming letter from one of the seminar attendees. Her letter really speaks for itself, so I will just pass it along to you:

I am fifty-eight years old and have never been married – on paper. I have had a friend that I fell in love with when we were fifteen years old. In fact, he was the one that convinced me that I needed to come to the Lord. We have not always lived a life victorious and free from immorality. He has been married many times and each time I prayed it would be me. I have always longed to be married and I have always felt so alone. As alone as I <u>felt</u>, my self-esteem did not have anywhere to fall.

Today after attending your seminar, I was walking alone along the beach just talking with God. I experienced one of the most beautiful days I can remember. I was talking to the Lord and telling Him how beautiful I found this gorgeous day. He said,

"Yes, it is beautiful, isn't it? But you are even more beautiful."

"Oh, no, not me Lord," I replied. "You know all the ugliness. You know all the failure, all the sins I commit, all the times I have asked you to forgive me and I go right back into the same sin. No Lord, you are mistaken. I am not beautiful. My mother told me no one would love me because I was fat and Lord you know I am still FAT."

As I continued to give Him all the reasons why I was not beautiful, He patiently waited for me to finish my argument. He then said, "I thought you beautiful enough to die for you."

Tears streamed down my face, out there on the beach alone with my Lord. I had no more argument but to believe that I am beautiful. He went on to tell me that being made in His image also meant that I was more beautiful than silver, more precious than gold, more valuable than diamonds – just as He is – because I am made in His image.

Finally, as if that were not enough, I began to pick up sand dollars on the beach. In the past whenever I have found sand dollars, they have always drawn me to the Creator and have given me a special 'connected' feeling. It is not often that I find whole ones, but as I continued to walk on the beach and converse with God, I began to find more and more whole sand dollars. One, two, five, and then would you believe twenty-five? I likened it to twenty-five pieces of silver that He paid to assure me I am beautiful. Wow! What a vivid illustration of His love.

This letter has been a powerful influence in my life. Can you identify with it too? How often do you put yourself down, feeling alone and ugly? You may need to realize that you are Christ's beloved. He sees you as His treasure and prize. He has paid dearly for you, but you are worth every pain He suffered. Possibly you need to recognize your worth to Him. Do not discount what He deems priceless. Let the truth surround you instead: you are His beloved.

The answer to loneliness lies not in human companionship, but rather in the spirit's communion with God. When you have the knowledge that He is truly one with you, loneliness will dissipate. You *are* loved. You do not have to keep wishing for it. You already have it. He loves you – truly and with full knowledge of who you are. Do not worry so much about how you have failed. To Him, you *are* beautiful as He looks through His eyes of Love.

"I don't mean to say I am perfect. I haven't learned all I should even yet, but I keep working toward that day when I will finally be all that Christ saved me for and wants me to be...I am still not all I should be but I am bringing all my energies to bear on this one thing: Forgetting the past and looking forward to what lies ahead."

Philippians 3:12-13

*"Let your roots grow down into him and
draw up nourishment from him,
See that you go on growing in the Lord,
and become strong and vigorous
in the truth you were taught.
Let your lives overflow with joy and
thanksgiving for all he has done."*

Colossians 2:7

We Have Come A Long Way, Baby

My daughter, Deanna, has always been such a challenge for me, even *before* she was born. I was nineteen years old, married for two months, and I had just found out I was one month pregnant. What a shock! I felt scared, delighted, and overwhelmed, but mostly delighted. I was young enough not to realize what was in store for me!

The last three months of my pregnancy were extremely difficult. I was in danger of miscarrying, so I had to quit my job, and lie flat on my back in bed. It is difficult for me to just sit still for an afternoon. Could I sit still for three months? In most instances I would have gone absolutely crazy with boredom and impatience. This time, however, I did not mind it too much. I had already fallen head-over-heels in love with my child. I would have endured much worse than bed rest in order to ensure a safe delivery. I should have taken it as a warning though—Deanna has been rearranging my life ever since!

Sometimes I cannot believe how fast time passes. I can remember my daughter's birth and childhood years as though they happened yesterday. Can the little curly-headed, blonde-haired girl of yesterday, be the green-eyed, beautiful brunette she is today? I can glimpse eternity when I realize that almost forty years have gone by in what seems like an instant.

I miss that little blonde girl, but I would not wish to have her back. Not that she was a naughty child. (Not *too* naughty anyway.) It is just that I enjoy the adult friendship and love that we share now. I would miss my grown-up friend more than I miss the little girl.

I wonder how many mothers feel as close to their adult daughters as I do. Every weekend, when I travel to women's groups to speak, I hear about estranged relationships. Whether it is estrangement from daughters, sons, spouses, sisters, brothers, mothers, fathers, the breakdown in relationships is prevalent. How thankful I am that Deanna and I have grown through our estrangements and continue to love and nurture each other.

Have Deanna and I been blessed? Or have we worked harder than some others to make our friendship grow? I suppose it is a little of both. I think mostly it is the fact that we do not place expectations on each other. We each allow the other to be who God intended us to be. It is just that simple and that difficult.

Who does not want to be in a relationship in which you are loved and accepted just the way you are? It is what all of us crave, but not what all of us receive or can give.

Is there someone in your life with whom you would like to have a better relationship? Try loving them unconditionally. I guarantee it will work.

Does unconditional love sound impossible to you? Maybe your relationships are so strained that it would take a miracle to restore them. Well, God can do miracles. He can help you to accomplish what seems impossible to you. *Permit* Him to do what seems impossible to you.

As you practice allowing God's love to flow through you to the other person, you and your relationships will be changed. I challenge you to give it a try. Only you can block the miracle-working Power.

"...May your roots go down deep into the soil of God's marvelous love; and may you be able to feel and understand, as all God's children should, how long, how wide, how deep, and how high his love really is; and to experience this love for yourselves, though it is so great that you will never see the end of it or fully know or understand it. And so at last you will be filled up with God himself."

Ephesians 3:17-19

Miss Thompson's Legacy

Since most of my extended family members are teachers, counselors, principals, or professors, I am often given educational stories that I enjoy immensely. This story, about Miss Thompson, has been told to me several times and I love it more every time I hear it.

Miss Thompson was a public school teacher who taught fifth grade. One day, Miss Thompson stood in front of all her students and said, "Boys and girls, I love you all the same. I have no favorites."

Of course, she was not being completely truthful. Teachers do have their favorites (we all do), and some teachers even have students they really do not like. For Miss Thompson, one such student was Teddy Stoulard.

Teddy did not like school. Each day he wore a deadpan facial expression and his eyes were glassy and unfocused. His appearance was unkempt, and his clothes were a mess. He never combed his hair and sometimes smelled horrible. When Miss Thompson tried to talk to Teddy, he always mumbled his response in monotone. He was a very unattractive boy when compared with many of the other children in the class.

According to Miss Thompson, she sometimes took a perverse pleasure in making a big checkmark beside Teddy's wrong answers. When she had to put an "F" for failure on the top of his paper, she would do it with flair. She should have been kinder, but with Teddy it was difficult.

One day, however, Miss Thompson read Teddy's file, which was kept in the school office. In each of the grades the following remarks were recorded:

First grade – Teddy shows promise with his work and attitude, but he has a poor home situation.

Second grade – Teddy could do better, but his mother is seriously ill. She receives little help at home.

Third grade – Teddy is a good boy, but too serious. He is a slow learner. His mother died last year.

Fourth grade – Teddy is very slow. He is well-behaved, but his father shows absolutely no interest in him.

It was almost Christmas, and the children began to bring gifts to school for their teacher. All the children in the class brought Miss Thompson beautiful gifts wrapped in bright Christmas paper with special bows and ribbons on them. To Miss Thompson's surprise, even Teddy brought a gift. It was wrapped in a brown paper bag and was held together with a little bit of scotch tape. On the top he had printed, "For Miss Thompson. From Teddy."

As Miss Thompson opened Teddy's gift, all the children were watching. Inside the bag was a gaudy rhinestone bracelet with half of the stones missing, and a used bottle of cheap perfume. The other children immediately began to laugh at Teddy's gift, but Miss Thompson put the bracelet on her wrist and daubed on a little of the perfume. She leaned down toward the children and said; "Doesn't it smell good? And look at how the bracelet sparkles!"

The children became quiet and stopped their laughter. Teddy looked above it all with his usual stone face.

When the school day was over, all of the children rushed out the door, but Teddy was the last to leave. Very slowly, he walked up to the front of the classroom and said, "Miss Thompson, you smell *just like my mom*. And her bracelet looks really pretty on you. I am glad you like my present."

Miss Thompson smiled at Teddy as he walked out the door and once she was alone she got on her knees and asked God to forgive her for her bad attitude.

The next day, those same children poured back into her classroom, but there was a different teacher there. Oh, her name was still Miss Thompson, but she was a different teacher. She had become a new person with a new attitude. She was no longer just a teacher, but somehow she also felt she was part of God's plan. In her heart she was now committed to loving her students more than she had ever done in the past, especially one particular student – a boy named Teddy.

By the end of the school year, Teddy showed dramatic improvement. He caught up with most of the other children and was even ahead of some of them. Miss Thompson passed him to the sixth grade with flying colors!

Several years later, Miss Thompson received an unexpected note from a young man named Teddy. It read:

"Dear Miss Thompson,

I wanted you to be the first to know. I will be graduating 2nd in my high school class.

Love,
Teddy Stoulard

Four more years passed and Miss Thompson received another note. It read:

41

Dear Miss Thompson,

I wanted you to be the first
to know. I just found out that I will
be graduating 1st in my class.
The university is not easy,
but I like it.

Love,
Teddy Stoulard

Four more years passed and Miss
Thompson received her third note. It read:

Dear Miss Thompson,

I wanted you to be the first
to know. As of today, I am Theodore
Stoulard, M.D. How about that?
I am getting married next month, the
27th to be exact. I want you to come
and sit where my mother would have
sat if she had been alive. You are my
only family. Dad died last year.

Love,
Teddy Stoulard

Of course Miss Thompson went to the
wedding. She realized how much her small
amount of love and care had meant to a lonely ten
year old boy. It had literally changed his life.

This lesson can apply to many areas in life.
Are you investing your love and care where it will

mean the most? Are you looking outside yourself for the people who desperately need someone to reach out to them?

Maybe you need to love and care for the woman at church who really bothers you, or a nosy neighbor, or even your own estranged son or daughter. Whoever it may be, is it time to forgive and ask God for a new attitude?

"Most important of all, continue to show deep love for each other, for love makes up for many of your faults."

I Peter 4:8

"God has given each of you some special abilities; be sure to use them to help each other, passing on to others God's many kinds of blessings."

I Peter 4:10

What Is Today's Agenda?

My father had a morning routine. Every morning he would walk from his bedroom down the hall to his study den, and begin his day in meditation time with the Lord. As a child I can remember all the times I watched him walk down that hall heading for his den. I never questioned it; it was just a regular part of my growing up years.

Now it has been over forty years since I was a child living with my parents, but I know that my father's morning routine continued with him until his death a few years ago. How do I know?

It happened several years ago when some of my family members, including my mother and father, decided to vacation together in Hawaii. One morning we were all gathered in the living room in an attempt to make plans for the day. My sister was finishing her coffee, my mother was collecting her handbag, and I was trying to get everyone out the door. In the midst of all the hullabaloo, someone said, "Well, are we ready to go?"

Quickly my father responded, "I'm ready! I have already gotten the agenda today from Upstairs!"

We all paused in our tracks and considered what he had said. With knowing smiles we realized that he was referring to his time spent with the Lord. Suddenly all of our "busyness" became less important. It was not *our* plans that mattered, but what the *Lord* had planned.

It is sometimes hard for me to wait on the Lord. I love to plan, supervise, and organize. I have come to realize, however, that God's plans are far superior to mine. Although it goes against my impatient nature, I know it is better to wait on the Lord and not miss out!

God has awesome and fabulous plans for you. Do you wait for Him? Do you get your daily agenda from "Upstairs"? Or do you miss countless blessings because you are oblivious to His plan for the day?

Lord, help me to consistently spend time with you. I want to be able to say, "I'm ready! I've gotten the agenda today from Upstairs!"

"Show me the path where I should go, O Lord; point out the right road for me to walk."

Psalm 25:4

45

"For I know the plans I have for you, says the Lord. They are plans for good and not for evil, to give you a future and a hope."

Jeremiah 29:11

Seal Up The Baggage

I was in an airplane at the Chicago O'Hare airport just as we were being pushed away from the gate for a scheduled departure. Suddenly the pilot came over the loudspeaker and said, "I wish I could give good news with this announcement, but I cannot. We have to go back to the gate because we have a problem with the baggage door. We cannot be on our way until the door is closed and sealed." The thought of all my baggage being strewn across the state of Illinois from thirty-five thousand feet made the pilot's suggestion sound like a good one! Although it meant a delay, I was quite happy with the idea of closing and sealing off the baggage door.

As the plane headed back to the gate, I started thinking about how we often carry baggage around in the storage compartment of our lives. We carry around the baggage of past mistakes,

47

past sins, relationship failures, bitterness, resentment, you name it. Many of us strew our baggage on everyone and anyone who comes in our path. We may find it impossible to completely close the baggage door by ourselves. Even when we think we have sealed the door some of the more rotten baggage may still seep out.

Maybe you have been carrying around the heavy baggage of failure, disappointment, or unresolved pain. Your life may be so full of this baggage that you cannot even begin to shut the door on it. Remember that what seems to you a heavy burden is to Christ a weightless feather. You do not burden Him to hand it over. If He is larger than the Universe – and He is – then He is certainly larger than your burden. You are struggling needlessly. Let Him seal up your past and help you move forward in your life as only He can.

By confessing your sins and shortcomings before God and asking for forgiveness you can be free from your burden. If you have asked Him to forgive you for the past He *will* forgive you. As it says in Colossians 2:13-14, "You were dead in sins, and your sinful desires were not yet cut away. Then he gave you a share in the very life of Christ, for he forgave all your sins, and blotted out the charges proved against you, the list of his commandments which you had not obeyed. He took this list of sins and destroyed it by nailing it to Christ's cross."

Since your sins were destroyed on Christ's cross, do not continue to let what is past destroy your future. The baggage door needs to be closed and sealed once and for all. Just like that airplane, you cannot leave the departure gate without it.

"He has put his seal upon us and given us his Spirit in our hearts as a guarantee."

II Corinthians 1:22 (RSV)

Why My Daughter Will Never Grow Up

Sometimes there are huge discrepancies in my relationship with my daughter, Deanna. On the one hand, we share a deep and mutual admiration. We work together with respect and friendship. On the other hand, she sometimes feels I am treating her as a child who needs her hand held to cross the street and I find myself still trying to shield her even though she is grown.

Deanna does not want me to shield her and we sometimes disagree about this issue. I have a difficult time accepting her grown up status, as you can tell by this recent conversation between us:

"Mom, there are days when I just want to shout, 'I am not a kid anymore!'" Deanna announced. "Do you see it, Mom? Look at me! I have gray in my hair. It has been over twenty years since I was in high school. Three of my own children are grown now. How can you still view me as a child?"

"No matter how old you are," I replied, "I am still twenty years older than you. What do you mean you are not a kid anymore? You are to me!"

"But, Mom," she continued, "I am capable of facing my own mistakes and consequences. I *want* to face them. I also want you to be proud that I am independent and strong. I really want to know that you recognize my growth."

"Well, I am sorry if I treat you like a child sometimes," I answered sincerely. "I do want to respect you and your feelings. I will *try* and remember that you *think* you are not a kid anymore. That is the best I can do! You will always be a kid to me!"

"Aaargh!" Deanna exclaimed. "I guess we will not have a resolution to this discussion in our lifetime. It is just one of those issues that I will have to accept and work around. I love you, Mom, but you can be *so exasperating!*"

In reality I know that Deanna is a grown woman. At least the *thinking* part of me knows it. The *feeling* part of me cannot grasp that she is anything other than my darling baby girl. Sometimes it is a real struggle for me to let the thinking part of me triumph over the feeling part. In my heart, I want to shield her. I do not want her to feel pain.

Do you ever experience the same sort of problem with your own children or family members? For me, it is one of life's hardest lessons – the learning to let go. It is especially difficult for me since I have always had the tendency to want to *fix* things. The phrase, "Mother knows best," really means something to me!

Of course, Deanna has her own words of wisdom for me. According to her, being an adult means taking your own risks and bearing the consequences of your choices. I know in my heart that she is right. I need to remember that Christ is in control of everything and my "control" is just in my own mind. In truth, only He has the ultimate control and authority for all of our lives.

"For the love of Christ controls us..."

II Corinthians 5:14 (RSV)

A Giving Heart

Several years ago I was invited to speak at a Pat Boone Celebrity Benefit for Bethel Bible Village, an organization that cares for children of prison inmates. It is a place where children can be sheltered, nurtured, and told about the love of Jesus Christ for them and their family. The children live in individual homes with house parents whom they call "aunt" and "uncle." No more than four to six children live in each home and it is a very loving and warm environment.

Pat Boone's annual event raises money for this wonderful charity and I felt honored to be the keynote speaker for the Saturday brunch during this special weekend. Many wealthy celebrities attended and I felt very excited and privileged to be able to share with them. Many people gave their money to help charity -- but *their* generosity is not what I remember about the weekend. I remember the generosity of Beverly.

Beverly was an eighteen year old girl living in one of the homes. She was not famous and certainly not wealthy. In fact, she had very few material possessions. What she did possess, however, was a thoughtful, loving, and very generous heart.

After speaking to the group of donors who attended the benefit, I was invited to tour the actual homes of some of the children. As Beverly gave me a tour of her bedroom, I looked around at her meager possessions. In the corner I noticed a shelf that held a small teddy bear collection. With great care and tenderness Beverly walked to the shelf and took down the most beautiful bear of them all, a new "Paddington Bear." Shyly, and with a sweet smile she lovingly put the teddy bear into my hands.

"Here, this is for you," she said.

Although my heart was instantly moved, I looked at her and said, "Thank you, Beverly, but I cannot take it."

Surprised, she looked at me and said, "Why not? I *gave* it to you."

I knew then that it was a gift I could not refuse, as it would have deprived her of joy. I recognized that it was important for her to receive the beauty and the blessing of giving. Besides, she had already known enough rejection in her past; she certainly did not need me rejecting her gift of love as well.

I hugged Beverly and she clung to me. We hugged for a long time. I thanked her for the beautiful gift and told her that it would always have a special place of honor in my home and in my heart. She beamed with joy.

Later that afternoon, before I left Bethel Bible Village, Beverly appeared at my side again. This time she had a little locket with her photograph in it. As she quietly slipped the locket around the teddy bear's neck my eyes filled with tears. I hugged her again as she whispered, "Please, do not forget me."

Beverly, I have not forgotten you. Not only did you teach me a valuable lesson, but the Lord has kept you present in my mind. Every time I look at your precious teddy bear and see the beautiful locket, I am reminded to pray for you. I know that wherever you are the Lord has a special plan for you and your generous heart. Not one of the wealthy celebrities I met that weekend can compare with you. Those famous people only gave a little from the large amount they had. You, however, gave so much from the little you had. Through you I have learned that an unselfish heart is the best kind of heart to have.

"For if you give, you will get! Your gift will return to you in full and overflowing measure, pressed down, shaken together to make room for more, and running over. Whatever measure you used to give – large or small – will be used to measure what is given back to you."

Luke 6:38

A New Future

My grandson, Robby, was born in Calcutta, India, and lived the first several years of his life with his birth parents. One day the whole city was preparing for an annual Hindu celebration. Statues of the Hindu gods were being paraded through the town and the streets were swarming with cars and people. Everyone was out having a good time, watching fireworks and celebrating. On that day Robby, then about five or six years old, was out on the streets with everyone else when his uncle drove past in a truck carrying one of the statues of the gods. Adults and children were climbing on the backs of the flatbed trucks as they drove slowly through the crowds, and Robby decided to join them. Feeling very independent and without consulting his parents, he scrambled onto the back of the truck.

Surrounded by many celebrants, all laughing and smiling, Robby thought this was one of the best days of his life. He felt sure that the truck would eventually bring him back by his house since his uncle was driving, so he was not worried.

Unfortunately, Robby had not counted on the size of the crowd, nor their jubilation and excitement. Many more people tried to climb on the truck as the parade made its way through the streets of Calcutta. At some point, quite a distance from Robby's home in an area of the city that he had never seen before, an excited celebrant accidentally pushed him off the end of the truck and into the teeming crowd. According to Robby's account, no one even noticed him fall; the truck never slowed down.

Suddenly thrown into an unfamiliar mass of people, Robby had no idea where he was or how to get home. Alone, frightened, and lost, he began crying for his parents. Someone on the street gave him a little money, and as night fell he had no choice but to curl up on the sidewalk and try to get some sleep.

In the morning, Robby's money was gone, stolen while he slept. Again he cried and finally attracted the attention of a passerby who took pity on him and told Robby he would help him get back to his parents. Robby went with the man to his home where the man called the police.

When the police arrived, they took Robby to a place where hundreds of other lost children are taken every year in India -- to a government run "home," which Robby refers to as "jail." Robby never saw his birth parents again. *In one night he lost his whole identity* -- his parents, brothers, sisters, his home, and any sense of security.

Everything familiar to him was taken away in an instant. For the next several years Robby lived in the children's "jails" in Calcutta. It was not until he was ten years old that Robby finally arrived in America to join our family.

I cannot even imagine the kind of loss that Robby has experienced. It is inconceivable to me. Yet Robby has continued to be optimistic and hopeful about the future. Yes, there are times when he still grieves for his birth family, but he has not allowed his past loss to cloud his new future. His smile, warmth, and love are freely given. He is a generous and inspiring young man who is learning how to let go of the things he cannot change.

Most of us, like Robby, need to let go of our painful past. We need to believe in a new future. Old slights, hurt feelings, wounded pride, even deeply painful wrongs, cannot be righted by holding onto them. Only letting them go can make things right again.

Whenever I am feeling particularly upset or depressed, I consider Robby. I have not even come close to suffering the way that he has suffered, so why am I complaining? The same can also be said when I think about what Christ suffered for me.

As one pastor once asked, "Have you suffered to the shedding of blood?"

"No."

"Then you are okay."

Christ suffered to the shedding of blood for you and me. Nobody has done anything to us like what our sin did to Him. That thought changes the whole perspective.

No matter how much forgiveness you extend, no matter how wide you open your arms to your enemy, no matter how far you spread your love, you can never match what Christ did for you. You are the receiver of His grace. Can you do less for yourself and others? Why not allow Him to give you a new future?

> *"For the Lord your God has arrived*
> *to live among you.*
> *He is a mighty Savior.*
> *He will give you victory.*
> *He will rejoice over you*
> *in great gladness;*
> *he will love you*
> *and not accuse you..."*

Zephaniah 3:17-18

No Mistake About It

My parents had four children. Keith is the oldest and my only brother. Next came my sister, Jean, my twin sister, Judy and then me. Judy is five minutes older than I am. In fact, when Judy was born they did not know I would be coming along at all. The doctors, nurses, and even my mother did not know there were twins. Our heartbeats were the same and in those days ultrasound was not readily available.

When Judy was born and everyone was thinking the birthing was over, my mom suddenly exclaimed, "I don't think I am through yet!" I came into the world as a total shock. Some would say I have been causing shock waves ever since!

I have been told that my dad almost fainted when he heard there were two of us; but his sister, my Auntie Doris, got very excited. Maybe that is why I have always felt close to Auntie Doris; she was the first person to welcome me into the world with whole-hearted enthusiasm!

Since I was often told about my shocking entry into this world, I grew up believing that I was a mistake. After all, no one was expecting my arrival to this earth. Well, no one, but God.

It was not until many years later that I could see God's plan for my life. I began to see that I was special and that my birth was not a shock to Him. He had planned and anticipated my arrival since before the beginning of time. What an awesome thought!

Do you feel that God must have made a big mistake when He made you? Nothing could be further from the truth.

"You made all the delicate, inner parts of my body, and knit them together in my mother's womb. Thank you for making me so wonderfully complex!
It is amazing to think about.
Your workmanship is marvelous--and how well I know it. You were there while I was being formed in utter seclusion!
You saw me before I was born and scheduled each day of my life before I began to breathe.
Every day was recorded in your Book!"

Psalm 139:13-16

Like No One Else

My twin sister, Judy, and I were so small when we first came home from the hospital that our heads could fit inside teacups. We were tiny and fragile, but for me, that would not last long! I quickly grew into a large-boned and tall person.

What I heard most often growing up was, "You are built just like your Aunt Nam." Well, Aunt Nam was built straight up and down, with no figure, just like a boy! My self-concept began to suffer right from the start.

How could I be built just like a big, strong, boy and feel good about myself as a girl? Since I had obviously lost out in the "looks" department, I would have to compensate in another area. Do you know what I did? I decided to develop my already naturally outgoing personality.

I was the enthusiastic, outspoken, maverick in a family of quiet, reserved, and decorous people. I stuck out like a sore thumb. You just could not miss me. I was tall, mischievous, and gregarious.

Just by my very existence, I turned our household on its ear. These are the messages I most remember from my childhood:

"Why can't you be more like your brother and sisters?"

"Don't do anything to hurt your father's name."

"Our church says you can't do that."

"What would other people think?"

I *could not* be like my brother and sisters. It was simply impossible although I really tried.

I also tried not to hurt my father's name, but it seemed that the slightest thing could besmirch it, so I blew that one too.

Likewise, our church had a low tolerance for the smallest infraction and I was always guilty of something.

As far as what other people would think? Well, I could not stop them from thinking, could I?

Growing up, it seemed like my whole life consisted of a list of *do's* and *don'ts*. I longed to know freedom, truth, and honesty, but I felt saddled with rules.

When I look back, I still marvel at the simplicity of God's truth. When I finally discovered my uniqueness and worth in God's sight it totally changed my life. No more rules, just these simple truths:

1. God loves and accepts me just the way I am.

2. He created me in His image.

3. He has a plan for my life.

4. I am unique and no one else can fulfill God's plan for my life.

5. I do not have to be perfect; I just need to allow God to work in and through me to daily conform my image to the image of Christ. This gives me the opportunity to be the best that I can be with what He's given me.

I would recommend that you memorize the above list in order to combat feelings of inadequacy and insecurity. Understanding my worth in God's eyes has changed my life. I am so glad that I am unique – even if I am built just like Aunt Nam!

"Let everyone be sure that he is doing his very best, for then he will have the personal satisfaction of work well done, and won't need to compare himself with someone else. Each of us must bear some faults and burdens of his own. For none of us is perfect."

Galatians 6:4-5

What's Your Name?

I have a friend, a pastor's wife, who is working on her own self-esteem issues. Her husband, the head pastor of their church, is a very outgoing, gregarious personality who enjoys greeting everyone after church. My friend is somewhat reserved, sometimes shy, and finds it hard to laugh freely. Lately she has been praying about gaining a better sense of humor and learning to relax more.

Today she called to tell me that the Lord was answering her prayers. At the end of last week's church service she and her husband were standing at the church door greeting people as they left. Since it is a growing church with a large congregation, there were many first-time people at the service. As each person came close to her husband he would reach out a hand to him or her and say, "Now, what's your name?" In the midst of all the people milling around him, he forgot that his wife was standing next to him. Without really looking at her, he then turned to his wife and said, "Now what's your name?" With a big smile on her face and a twinkle in her eye she sweetly replied, "Remember, I'm the one you slept with last night."

Peals of laughter were heard from the regular attendees who had gathered around the newcomers. Her husband looked slightly shocked and completely taken by surprise. As quickly as he could recover his senses, he started assuring everyone that she was his wife!

My friend told me about how good it felt to be able to have a sense of humor and tease her husband. She walked around the rest of that day feeling better about herself. Her husband, although surprised at this new side of his usually shy wife, has been delighted to see her relax. They have been laughing together about the incident and they both have a new appreciation for the other.

What about you? Do you need to relax and find a sense of humor? Would you like to be free to truly be yourself? Would you like to feel light and carefree – able to find and express true joy and love?

Christ wants to help you with all of this. He wants you to know the joy of being you. He has created you in a wondrous fashion; He wants you to believe this and let it free you. Allow your sense of humor, your own God-given personality, to be evident in all that you do.

Maybe you are like the caterpillar that was once bound up in a tight cocoon suddenly discovering that you now have wings, freedom, and the ability to fly. At first, the sense of space and freedom from confinement may feel strange. There is no sin, however, in enjoying your freedom and lightness of being. You do not need a heavy coating of piousness to be spiritual. Laugh, smile, giggle – unleash your joy. Having a relationship with Jesus Christ should be permeated with this hard-to-contain joy. Go ahead -- express who you are in His love!

"...you have been given freedom:
not freedom to do wrong,
but freedom to love
and serve each other."

Galatians 5:13

I Could Use Some Help!

DAILY PRAYER:

So far today, God,
I've done all right...
I haven't gossiped.
I haven't been grumpy, nasty or selfish.
I'm really glad of that,
but in a few minutes, God,
I'm going to get out of bed.
From now on, I'm probably going to
need a lot of help.

I can sure identify with the above prayer.
Can you? Yes, it makes me chuckle, but the truth
also hits home.

When we gossip, act grumpy, nasty or
selfish, we are not honoring the Lord or our fellow

human beings. Maybe it is time to consider asking the Lord's help so we can get up on the right side of the bed!

"Don't just pretend that you love others: really love them. Hate what is wrong. Stand on the side of the good. Love each other with brotherly affection and take delight in honoring each other."

Romans 12:9-10

The *Christkind* Miracle

My friend, Doris Pitman, grew up in Kirchberg, Germany. She was born to a German mother and French father at the end of World War II. She grew up never knowing her father as he abandoned her mother before Doris was born. Her life in Germany after World War II was poverty-stricken and desolate.

As an adult, Doris came to have a personal relationship with Christ and was responsible for winning many other people to Him during her lifetime. Although Doris died a few years ago from cancer, she left a rich legacy for her family and friends to remember. Here, in her own words, is one of my favorite stories about Doris:

As a child I wanted to escape my terrible circumstances, but I could never deny that God was watching over me. There were many times throughout the years when His guiding hand was very apparent. One instance, in particular, is a vivid example of His overwhelming love and goodness to me even in the midst of my distress and poverty. He showed me that He never forgets His children.

It happened when I was about ten years old. It was in December and everyone was getting ready for Christmas. My mother, sister, and I took the train from Kirchberg to visit my aunt and cousins in Koblenz. We stayed there a couple of days and decided to go into town to look at all the Christmas decorations in the store windows. This was a very big treat for us.

It was night and there was snow all over the ground. It was very cold and quite a long walk into town from my aunt's house. All of this was forgotten, however, when we arrived in front of a toy store's window that was decorated and full of dolls.

At the time, my dream was to someday have a baby doll. The only doll I owned was one that my mother had put together for me. She had found an old beat-up doll body and then bought a new head for it. I loved the doll, but it had straight legs and was a grown-up doll. I wanted a cuddly baby doll.

I can remember it as if it happened yesterday. I was standing at the store window looking at all the dolls when I saw a baby doll that had fallen forward and seemed to be reaching out its hand to me. I cried out to my mother, "Oh, mama, look! That doll is reaching out to me. It wants to come to me. That is the doll I want! Oh, I want that doll! Do you think that Christkind (the Christ child) could bring this doll to me?"

71

My mother was silent. She knew, just as I did, that there was not really a Santa Claus or a magical Christkind who would bring the doll to me. I was old enough to know that if I were going to get the doll, my mother would have to buy it for me. Still I continued to plead with her, "Do you think I could get a doll like that?"

My mother looked at the price tag on the doll. It cost a quarter of my mother's monthly income. My mother knew that it was impossible. With tears in her eyes, she looked at me and said, "You know that I would love to buy this for you, but I just do not have the money. I am so sorry."

I understood what my mother was saying, but my disappointment was crushing. I cried and cried inconsolably. As the days went by I could not stop thinking about the doll and each time I would think about it I would begin to cry again. It was exactly the one doll that I had dreamed of owning. It was a real baby doll with a little blue and white suit and a pacifier in its mouth. I longed for it constantly.

About two weeks went by and it was getting close to Christmas. I came home from school one day and my mother seemed very excited. This was a big departure from her usual sadness. With a big smile she said, "Look what I have here!" It was a letter of invitation from the American soldiers stationed at Hahn Air Force Base about eight miles outside Kirchberg. The Americans were planning a party for just a select group of children. They chose children who did not have a father, had lost parents in the war, or were very poor. For once in my life, my sad circumstances worked in my favor! I could not believe they had chosen me for this special event! It seemed that only the bad things happened to our family, but in this case, something good was happening. It made for a very festive week in our household.

The party was the following Saturday and the Americans had reserved the local theater for the party to be held there. I can remember that party so clearly. Soldiers in uniform were everywhere; some with their wives, and the place looked beautiful. There were huge Christmas trees all around and huge American cakes with icing on them. There was fruit and just so much food! I thought I must be in paradise. It was so overwhelming; I had never seen anything like it in my life.

My mother and I enjoyed looking around and then sat at a table together. When we sat down, someone brought us hot cocoa with big white marshmallows. It was the first time I had seen marshmallows. It was wonderful!

I could not believe the abundance of food they provided for us, even things that were usually scarce. One of those foods was a luxury called a banana. My mother could never afford to buy them, but that night I ate my first banana. The whole evening was more than my child's mind could comprehend. It was heaven on earth to me.

As a grand finale to this glorious party, someone got up on the theater stage and announced that Santa Claus was coming out. There were two Christmas trees on stage and two huge sacks of wrapped gifts. In addition, two women helped

Santa by calling the children up one by one. From the large bag of wrapped gifts Santa Claus randomly chose one and lovingly presented it as each child stepped forward. Suddenly, I began to feel very shy.

"I am not going up there," I told my mother, "you will have to go with me."

"Look," my mother replied, "all the other kids are going up. You can do it. All you have to do is walk up the stairs, get your present and tell Santa Claus, 'Danke' (thank you)."

"I am too scared to go up there. Please go with me," I pleaded.

"I know you can do it," my mother answered.

Our back and forth discussion continued as the list of children's names continued to be called out. I kept protesting and my mother kept reassuring. Finally, they called my name and I had to go. My mother stayed in her seat and I walked to the stage alone. My heart was beating so hard I really thought I might die and I was literally shaking. Very slowly I walked up the stairs, received my gift from Santa Claus and said, "Danke."

When I walked back to my table I sat down next to my mother. She took one look at the box and said, "Oh, I hope it is a pair of boots!" It was true that I needed a pair of boots, but it was not what I wanted to hear.

"I will open it up later," I said.

"Open it up now," my mother urged.

"No, I am going to open it up at home."

"No, Doris, you need to open it up now. All the other kids are opening their presents. You need to open yours too."

With the utmost reluctance I started to open my present. I was afraid it was going to be a pair of boots and I would be disappointed. I carefully unwrapped the box, looked inside, and then I just screamed. I was so loud that everyone came rushing over to see what was wrong with me. They crowded around saying, "What is wrong? Is everything okay?"

I could not answer. I just looked up at my mother with tears streaming down my face. The gift inside the box was the very same baby doll I had seen in the window display. It was the exact same doll.

Finally I found my voice and said to my mother, "You see, the Christkind really did bring me the doll!"

"You are the God of miracles and wonders! You still demonstrate your awesome power."

Psalm 77:14

75

Listening For God's Voice

God desires that we not only *talk* to Him, but also *listen* to Him. He wants a relationship with us that is a two-way street. Can you hear God's voice? Do you know what it sounds like in your heart? Sometimes it just takes practice and training to really know *for what* to listen.

A Midwestern young farmer came to visit his former college roommate in New York City. As they were walking near Times Square, the farmer suddenly said, "I hear a cricket!"

"You are crazy," replied his friend, "it is the rush hour here in New York and there is no way you can hear a cricket!"

"No, I did hear a cricket," said the young farmer as he walked to the corner. Listening intently he then crossed the busy avenue and looked all around. Finally he walked to a shrub that was growing in a large cement planter.

Digging around under the shrub, he found his cricket.

Turning to his New York friend he said, "My ears are no different than yours. It simply depends *for what* you have learned to listen. Here, let me show you."

Reaching into his pants' pocket, he pulled out a handful of change. Looking around at the crowd pushing past him, he slowly dropped the coins on the sidewalk. At the sound of money hitting the pavement, every head turned.

"See what I mean?" asked the farmer, "It all depends *for what* you have learned to listen."

For what have you learned to listen? Can you hear God's voice as a small whisper in your heart? Can you hear His voice in the Scriptures as you read them? Maybe you need to train your ears to recognize God's voice. What God has to say to you is very important. Let Him teach you *for what* to listen.

"Come to me with your ears wide open. Listen, for the life of your soul is at stake..."

Isaiah 55:3

When Mothers Need Comforting

My father's death was imminent. His last request was that he be allowed to die at home surrounded by people he loved. My mother, brother, sisters and I, along with our spouses and children, spent the last weeks of my father's life caring for him at my parent's home. A hospital bed was brought into the living room of the house and we each took our turns sitting beside, watching over, and visiting with Dad.

My father was dying and I was very worried about my mother. My parents had been married for sixty-two years and had never been separated for any length of time. My mother felt that her whole world was dying with my father. The pain and the grief were unbearable.

In the weeks before his death, my mother and I had many conversations similar to this one:

"Joanne, how can I survive without your father? The pain and the loneliness of facing life without him are too great."

"I know, Mother. I wish so much that I could take the hurt away, but I cannot. Instead, I will pray for God to bring you His peace."

"That is just it, Joanne. Right now I do not feel God's presence or His peace. What I feel is *terror*. I am absolutely terrified when I think about a future without your father beside me."

What could I do to help? My mother, who was often a comfort for me, needed my comfort now. I wanted to fix it for her, to somehow make it better. I felt powerless and defeated; all I could do was pray.

That last Saturday we all knew Dad would soon be heaven bound; he had slipped into a coma-like state and was not responsive to us anymore. That afternoon my mother requested time alone with Dad. As she sat beside his bed, talking softly to him, she was suddenly consumed with the *terror*. Frantically, she began to thrash about in her mind for the answer to her fear, but she could find no relief. The fear became so overwhelming she did not know if she could survive it.

At that moment, a soft, gray, mist-like cloud moved over her and filled the room. Puzzled, my mother turned around to look through the large window behind her. Could a dark cloud have cast a shadow over the sun?

Outside, the sky was bright blue. It was one of those beautiful, clear, and sun-filled days, not a cloud to be seen. Inside, the mist-cloud began to swirl around and envelop my mother in its comforting presence. The most wonderful peace settled into her heart and mind. God spoke to her in the stillness of her heart and said, "It is going to be okay." With a fresh sense of courage, my mother knew that it was true.

The comfort that enveloped my mother stayed with her the rest of the day. It stayed with her the next morning as she sat beside my father when he took his last breath. It remained with her in the days afterwards. The memory of it remains with her still.

I now realize that God, in His great love, answered my prayer. He knew that I could not fix my mother's pain and terror; only He could. I also have confirmation that God sends His Holy Spirit to comfort the grieving. The Comforter is *always* with us.

I am learning not to feel defeated when all I can do is pray. In reality, all I *need* to do is pray!

"Be strong and courageous. Do not be afraid or terrified...for the Lord your God goes with you; he will never leave you nor forsake you."

Deuteronomy 31:6 (NIV)

The Universal Language

I have just finished reading an article about the growing research supporting the power of touch. Although I have been an advocate of touch for many years, it was good to be reminded of just how important touch can be for our well being. Experts say that we need four hugs a day just to survive, eight hugs to maintain, and twelve hugs to grow.

My granddaughter, Kimmi, was adopted from Korea at the age of two and a half years old. She came not speaking or understanding any English and was also unaware of how to give or receive hugs and kisses. She literally had to be shown how to wrap her arms around someone and how to pucker her lips.

Within two weeks of her arrival, however, she was hugging and kissing everyone in sight. It was her greatest joy and to this day (fifteen years later) she still loves to hug and kiss her family as much as she can.

Thinking about touch brings the image of Mother Teresa to my mind. I see her working in the slums of Calcutta, reaching out and touching the "untouchable." With her outstretched arms, she manifested Christ's love to dying individuals.

The Bible often talks about how Jesus *touched* others. He did not just heal them with his words, he *touched* them and then they were healed. The Bible also tells us that Jesus laid His hands on the little children who were brought to Him for a blessing. He could have stood at a distance and blessed them with His words, but instead He gathered them into his arms in a loving embrace. To me, it illustrates just how important appropriate touch should be to all of us.

It is not always enough to tell someone you care. Often your warm embrace can convey the meaning much better. Why not try it out on those you love?

"Then he took the children into his arms and placed his hands on their heads and he blessed them."

Mark 10:16

Do Not Walk Outside This Area

I was in an airplane flying thirty-five thousand feet over Canada when I looked out the window and saw a sign printed on the wing of the plane. It read, "Do not walk outside this area."

No chance! I thought. *You will never catch me walking outside this airplane at thirty-five thousand feet. I will stay right here in my seat!*

Although I quickly realized the sign was for the ground crew when the plane had landed safely and parked at the gate, I chuckled to myself nonetheless. As I looked again I realized that the sign included a big, red-bordered area marking the correct place for the ground crew to walk. It reminded me of how many times I have read, taught, and heard God's Word and learned all about the warning signs and boundaries for my life only to disregard the red-border and His warning not to "walk outside this area."

Have you ever done this? Are you one of those people that will deliberately walk on a lawn that has a posted sign saying, "Keep off the grass"? Do you like to do just the opposite of what you know is good for you? Are you a rebel with or without a cause?

A rebellious spirit needs to be addressed. Boundaries are there for a reason. When you learn to respect boundaries you will be surprised at how it increases freedom and reduces rebellion.

Living outside of God's boundaries for us can lead to certain death, just like walking on the wing of an airplane at thirty-five thousand feet. Do not believe the lie that rebellion brings freedom. In truth, rebellion brings slavery and bondage. Only obeying Christ's warning signs and following His boundaries for our lives can bring freedom.

If you are a rebel, remember that Christ does not want to *conquer* you. Instead, He came to set you free.

"You are free from the law, but that doesn't mean you are free to do wrong. Live as those who are free to do only God's will at all times."

I Peter 2:16

Will The Real Joanne Wallace Please Stand Up?

I had always had this funny idea that I would like to meet some other Joanne Wallace. I had met thousands and thousands of women during my speaking career, but I had never met another Joanne Wallace. I used to search the telephone books in all of the different cities where I was speaking each weekend just hoping to find another Joanne Wallace. I found a Joan Wallace, Jan Wallace, Jean Wallace...but never a Joanne Wallace.

When I moved to California in the late 1980's, I was still searching for another Joanne Wallace. Since I was new to the city of Fremont, I decided to look in the phone book. With great surprise, I found two other Joanne Wallaces listed! There were three of us in the same community!

Of course, I could not just leave it at that; I had to call them both. It was really quite delightful. Imagine the conversation:

"Hello."

"Hello. This is Joanne Wallace. Is Joanne Wallace there?"

Both of the other Joanne Wallaces are such fun people – almost as crazy as I am! In fact, it was so enjoyable talking with them that we decided we should all meet each other. A few weeks after our first conversation, I called both of them back and we set up a time to get together for lunch. The only problem was that we could not decide which name to use when making the restaurant reservation!

Over lunch the three Joanne Wallaces had a hilarious time. We talked for several hours and found out that we had so much in common. We were all about the same age; had all been through some deep personal losses and pain; and we were all born-again Christians! Of course we knew that God had planned for us to meet and become friends, but just think what a blessing we all would have missed if I had not made those first calls.

Sometimes when a fresh idea or sudden inspiration comes to us we just need to act on it. It took me fifty-some years to finally fulfill my dream of meeting another Joanne Wallace, but it was worth the wait.

What do you dream about? Do you have any great ideas that need fulfilling?

....

"Be delighted with the Lord. Then he will give you all your heart's desires."

Psalm 37: 4

Dear Diary

Sometimes life gets too complicated and it is fun to reflect back to simpler times. Just recently, Deanna shared with me some of the humorous excerpts from her sixth grade diary. It made me chuckle and refreshed my day. I hope it does the same for you.

The year was 1970, Deanna was eleven years old, and here is what she had to say about the following subjects:

FAMILY

Jan. 11   *Tonight we have family night where we do something as a family. Who knows what.*

Jan. 19   *It's Monday and I'm glad to be alive. (I have times to want to live, you know.)*

Feb. 28   *Did fun thing today with Mom and Dad. We started to fly a kite. Didn't get very far.*

SCHOOL

Mar. 29   *Today, school again, and many other things of non-importance.*

Mar. 30   *School, school, school. I wish I didn't have to go to it. Sort of.*

BOYS

Jan. 26   *Went skating with Anita (my friend) today. She met a boy named Robert. He called her twice and she hates him.*

April 18   *Stayed all night at Anita's. We talked about who we liked and all the times we'd talked to that boy. Oh, yeah, astronauts of Apollo 13 got back safe.*

April 30   *Talked to Jon Urhammer and I think he likes me. I like him.*

May 8   *Jon Urhammer sat by me today. He did it all by himself and not because he had to.*

Oh, to be an eleven year old again! Life was so much simpler!

"...for the joy of the Lord is your strength. You must not be dejected and sad!"

Nehemiah 8:10

89

Never Too Late

At a speaking engagement in Florida, I had the wonderful privilege of meeting a woman who had lived to be ninety-three years of age. She came up to the book table during the lunch break and asked me to sign one of my books. I was happy to oblige, but felt a deep urgency in my spirit that the Lord had more than a book signing in mind.

As this dear woman stood waiting for me to finish signing the book, she related that she had not been to church in thirty years. She was currently attending Al-Anon meetings and believed in a Higher Power, but she did not have a personal relationship with Jesus Christ. Hearing her speak, I looked up into the tired, wrinkled, and intelligent face of a woman who was finally ready to turn her life over to God. When I asked her if she would like to know the Higher Power on a more personal level, she nodded in agreement. Immediately, I stood up, put my arm around her and led her in a simple prayer to ask Jesus into her heart and life.

The whole exchange took about sixty seconds, but it was enough time to totally change her future. No matter how much time she has left on this earth, when she does leave she will find a new life in heaven!

"And all who trust him—God's Son—to save them have eternal life; those who don't believe and obey him shall never see heaven, but the wrath of God remains upon them."

John 3:36

Only God's Planning

In the field of professional speaking, there is no greater honor than to receive the coveted Council of Peers Award for Excellence (CPAE) Speaker Hall of Fame designation from the National Speakers Association (NSA). To a professional speaker, the CPAE Speaker Hall of Fame is the equivalent of an actor's Academy Award.

In one calendar year, the National Speakers' Association awards only five CPAE Speaker Hall of Fame winners out of a possible field of over four thousand members. The criteria for receiving the award are very demanding and the nomination and ultimate review by the executive committee is intense. For many years I have enjoyed going to the annual CPAE award ceremony, but never dreamed I would be chosen to receive this high honor.

I was absolutely stunned when I received a call several months before the 1996 award ceremony telling me that I had been chosen to receive one of the five CPAE Speaker Hall of Fame awards for that year! I was instructed not to tell anyone about my award, but to prepare a speech to give at the banquet and to send the planning committee a musical selection on compact disc of my favorite song. The song was to be played when my name was announced and I walked to the platform at the award ceremony.

My mind started racing one hundred miles per hour. I tried to think of what song I wanted to play as my "theme song." I knew that I wanted to bring glory to the Lord by my selection, but I also wanted to find a song that could be easily identified by the two thousand guests (mostly secular speakers), who would be attending the ceremony. Finally, I decided on one of my favorite songs, *Amazing Grace*. The first verse goes like this:

Amazing grace, how sweet the sound
That saved a wretch like me.
I once was lost, but now am found,
Was blind, but now I see.

I knew I could start my testimony with that song, but also that it had been popular in the secular market at one time. I felt it would be the perfect choice for a very special event.

I looked forward to the award ceremony for months, but *of course*, the week before the ceremony, I became very ill with a sinus and bronchial infection. Although the doctor put me on strong antibiotics, I still became the proud owner of the deepest, harshest, and loudest chest cough of my life. It was a blaring cough straight out of my worst nightmare; one that could cause major hearing loss to anyone within a fifty mile radius of my vicinity. I am fully convinced that those unfortunate souls who actually heard my cough are still talking about it today. Some of the people around me had to hold their ears because it hurt *them* just to hear *me*. I knew that if I coughed into the microphone during my acceptance speech the guests would run for the exit door thinking a bomb was going off!

For a public speaker, it was a disastrous cough, but I refused to panic. I just kept praying for the Lord to touch me and for His will to be done.

When the day finally arrived for the award ceremony, my cough was worse than before. I realized, however, that God was in control and I would just have to trust Him for the outcome. As I sat at the banquet table eating dinner with my husband, daughter, son, sister, and brother-in-law, I was remarkably relaxed.

Half way through the first course, I felt a soft tap on my shoulder. Looking around, I saw the woman in charge of the program standing there with an empty compact disc case in her hand. Quietly she explained to me that this was the compact disc case I had given her for *Amazing Grace*, but the compact disc was not actually in the case.

I just could not believe it! How could the compact disc have gotten lost? I did not have any time to panic though, because I was scheduled to receive my award within thirty minutes and I had to come up with a new musical number on the spot. With no time to waste, Deanna and I went back to the sound booth and we hastily picked out a peppy, secular instrumental. Although I was not really thrilled with it, it was the best choice we could make from the available selection of secular artists.

As Deanna and I made our way back to the dinner table, I silently prayed that God would have His way. I was disappointed that I would not be able to start out my speech with my chosen song, but I knew the Lord could work all situations for good because I was trusting in Him. Besides, my cough was enough to worry about!

Finally the moment came when my good friend, Naomi Rhode, stood on the platform to introduce me and present me with my award. (Naomi is a past president of NSA, a wonderful Christian speaker, the utmost in excellence in speaking, and she had previously received the CPAE award.) As Naomi introduced me, she casually mentioned that my original choice of *Amazing Grace* as my opening song had been lost.

As Naomi officially announced my name, the spotlight hit my face. I hugged my family and started making my way through the crowd to receive my "Oscar." The peppy secular number I had selected was playing in the background and after I had climbed the stairs to the stage, Naomi hugged me and handed me the award trophy.

Just as the instrumental music died down, I heard the most beautiful and angelic voice start to sing, "Amazing grace, how sweet the sound..." There, in the front of the room was my friend, Liz Curtis Higgs, (a fantastic Christian speaker and author, plus a past CPAE recipient) standing up at her table singing "my" song. As I listened in utter amazement, a hush fell over the group and a man from Scotland stood up with his bagpipes and started to play accompaniment. I heard the great swelling of voices as everyone in the audience joined in too. The room became filled with the sweet, precious, and inspiring words of *Amazing Grace*. It was a tremendously moving and humbling experience – one that only God could have orchestrated!

As I stood at the podium, listening to the crowd sing about God's grace, I knew that God had planned this moment all along. He wanted everyone's attention to be fully focused on Him, and in this He succeeded!

There was a reverence in the room when I began my acceptance speech, and guess what? I did not cough even once while I was on the platform! I talked for about ten minutes and thanked all of the supporting people in my life, recounting part of my journey that led me to that very moment. As a conclusion to my talk, I then spoke from my heart and said, "I want everyone to know that I am committed to Jesus Christ. It makes no difference your age, color, social status, nationality, or creed, I long to tell everyone that God so loved the world that He gave His only Son to die for us. God thinks that all people are worth that; and that is good news!"

As I walked back to the table after giving my speech, I realized that I had just experienced God's incredible power in action. The feelings of that moment are unforgettable!

I was later told that my message might have been the first time anyone had clearly presented the gospel of Christ in a large assembly of the National Speakers Association. Isn't that just like God? He will take the frailest vessel (like me with my cough), the worst set of circumstances (like a lost compact disc), and turn it into the most awesome and glorious time for Him. His plans are always better than mine are, and if I surrender to His will, then His plans can be accomplished through me.

Every time I am upset or frustrated by my circumstances, or discouraged by my failures, I remember God's power in using what I perceive to be problems in order to accomplish His plan. God, in His desire to reach us with Christ's love, is indeed more powerful than we can even imagine.

"Let everyone in all the world – men, women and children – fear the Lord and stand in awe of him. For when he but spoke, the world began! It appeared at his command! And with a breath he can scatter the plans of all the nations who oppose him, but his own plan stands forever..."

Psalm 33:8-11

Equally Ordinary

We are all equally ordinary. Yes, I know that some people may disagree with me, but I believe that if we are *really* honest with ourselves we will admit that all of us have good points and bad points. It is only through an extraordinary God that we become transformed. Fortunately for all of us, God has chosen to use ordinary people to fulfill His extraordinary plans.

Maybe you have a secret list of all the reasons why God could not and should not use you. You may even feel you are less than ordinary. If so, you can take heart today because you are in good company. Just take a look at this list:

Moses stuttered.
David's armor didn't fit.
John Mark was rejected by Paul.
Timothy had ulcers.
Hosea's wife was a prostitute.

Amos' only training was in the school of fig tree
pruning!
Jacob was a liar.
David had an adulterous affair.
Abraham was too old.
David was too young.
Peter was afraid of death.
Lazarus was dead.
John was self-righteous.
Naomi was a widow.
Paul was a murderer...so was Moses.
Jonah ran away from God.
Miriam was a gossip.
Gideon and Thomas both doubted.
Jeremiah was depressed and suicidal.
Elijah was burned out.
John the Baptist was a loudmouth.
Martha was a worrywart.
Mary was lazy.
Samson had long hair.
Noah got drunk.
Did I mention that Moses had a short fuse?
So did Peter, Paul, -- well, lots of folks.

We are all ordinary people with our own
faults and hang-ups, but it is precisely in our
ordinariness that God's extra-ordinariness can be
manifested. In our weakness, His strength is
shown. Barbara Johnson, in her monthly
newsletter stated that "if you are magically in love
with Him and you long for Him more than you do
your next breath, He will use you regardless of

who you are, where you have been, or what you look like."

As an ordinary person, God wants you to accept yourself (with all your limitations) so that He can do extraordinary things through you. If you feel weak, limited, ordinary, you are the best material through which God can work. Why not give Him permission to use you?

*"Notice among yourselves,
dear brothers, that few of you
who follow Christ have big names
or power or wealth. Instead, God has
deliberately chosen to use ideas
the world considers foolish and of little
worth in order to shame those
people considered by the world
as wise and great."*

I Corinthians 1:26-27

Living Without Regrets

Deanna decided to live her life without regrets when she was just fourteen years old. It is a commitment that has stayed with her for the last twenty-five years. Even today, she goes to sleep at night with a clear conscience and a light heart because she knows she has peace with all of her loved ones.

Deanna's lesson began on a Monday in December, 1972. On that day, her friend, Laurie Paschall, a school cheerleader, asked Deanna to stay after school with her to help make hand-painted posters for the basketball game and pep rally. Best friends since they were both three years old, they had not spent much time together recently. It was the perfect opportunity for the teenagers to visit with each other and also do something productive.

That afternoon Laurie and Deanna painted, laughed, and reminisced with each other for hours. They talked about everything they could remember from their childhood years together and had so much fun. They recalled church camps, silly songs they had performed, and how God had been so good at keeping them close together through the years. It was one of those afternoons that left them both feeling satisfied and content. As they reaffirmed their friendship and love for each other, neither one realized it would be the last time they would see each other on this earth.

The very next day it began to snow. Just a little bit at first, but then much harder. Soon it was falling fast and furious, piling up several inches in just a few hours. By the end of the day, school was canceled as the snowstorm hit with full force. Everyone scrambled to get home before they were stuck on campus for the duration of the storm.

The snowstorm continued for several more days with no school. By Friday, the storm had finally let up and people were outside building snowmen, having snowball fights, and enjoying the opportunity for sledding. It was also a great opportunity to enjoy being at home, with no homework, curled up in bed with a good book.

That is exactly what Deanna was doing when the phone rang. It was her friend, Kerri, calling with bad news:

"Deanna, my mom works at the emergency room of the hospital and they just brought Laurie in. She had some kind of accident while sledding."

"How bad is she hurt? Did she sprain her foot or break a leg?"

"I don't know. My mom just called to tell me they had brought her in, so I decided to call you."

"Okay, well, thanks for letting me know."

As Deanna hung up the phone her heart was seized with panic. She just knew that something was terribly wrong with Laurie. It was not a broken leg or sprained ankle. Something told her she needed to get to the hospital immediately.

Deanna ran up the stairs from her bedroom and began shouting, "Dad, Dad, come quickly. You have got to take me down to Memorial Hospital. Laurie has been in an accident and they have taken her to the emergency room. Come on, Dad, we have to go *now!*"

Usually, her Dad would have argued with her. After all, the roads were still difficult to maneuver because of the snow and there was no information that would lead him to believe the situation was urgent. His normal instinct would be to just wait and see what could be found out over the telephone. This time, however, he seemed to pick up Deanna's urgency. She was insistent and determined to get to that hospital.

By the time they arrived at the hospital, Deanna's heart was filled with dread. She walked into a small, private, waiting room and saw Laurie's cousins, Sam and Jim, sitting there. They all looked at each other mutely. No one knew what to say. There was a sadness and fear that permeated the atmosphere. Just then, the doctor walked into the room. He looked at the three teenagers and simply said, "Laurie is gone. We had her on the operating table, but we were unable to repair the damage."

Sam and Jim tried to fill Deanna in on the details. Laurie and a group of family and friends had decided to spend the morning sledding and inner tubing on the hill above Laurie's home. Everything had gone well until Laurie took her last ride down the hill on an inner tube. As she came flying down the hill she ran into a small tree. In fact, it was just a sapling, because it bent over when she hit it. This sapling, however, caught Laurie across the chest and caused major internal damage. Her spleen was ruptured and the aorta was torn from her heart. She died within two hours of the accident.

God did not save Laurie's life on that operating table and to Deanna that seemed to be very unfair. It is often hard to understand God's reasons and timing for tragic events, especially if you are the one left behind when a loved one dies.

For Deanna, it was important to see God as part of the healing process when sorrow came. God is not the author of the sorrow, but He can be the author of the healing for the sorrow.

Through time, Deanna was able to see God's hand of blessing in the time He allowed her to spend with Laurie just days before her death. It was very healing to know that she and Laurie had had a chance to reaffirm their friendship and love the last time they had been together. Deanna was able to see God's merciful hand in this situation and it has made all the difference in her life since that time.

Through the tragedy of Laurie's death, Deanna formulated the conviction that she did not want to live one day with regrets. From the age of fourteen onward she has not forgotten her conviction. She does not leave loving words unsaid or forgiveness unasked. She has truly learned the lesson of living one day at a time as though it were the last.

Have you learned that lesson yet?

"Teach us to number our days
and recognize how few they are;
help us to spend them as we should."

Psalm 90:12

"Everything is appropriate in its own time.
But though God has planted eternity in the
hearts of men, even so, many
cannot see the whole scope of God's work
from beginning to end."

Ecclesiastes 3:11

Listing All The People Who Like You

When my grandson, Aron, was three years old, he came to visit me. Sitting on my sofa one day, he suddenly began to recite people's names. He seemed to be contemplating each name as he said, "Mommy, Daddy, Grandma, Grandpa, Jesse, Erika, Brooke..."

Puzzled, I interrupted him and asked, "Aron, what are you doing?"

He looked at me, surprised that I should even ask such a question, and proudly said, "I am listing all the people who like me!"

His response confirmed what I believe about human nature. We all need to be assured that we are loved and accepted. It does not matter who you are, but it does matter how you feel about

106

yourself. Self-acceptance is the foundation of confidence.

So who do you include on your list of people who like you? I hope that the very top of your list reads, "God."

It is true. God loves you just the way you are. He loves even the things you cannot change. He loves you, imperfections and all. He wants to use you and flow through you to others. Your ultimate worth is based on that which is eternal – God. Knowing this, believing this, will result in the assurance that you are loved and accepted as you are. So, get your list out and remember that God is one of the people who likes you! I can think of no better basis for living life with confidence!

"But God showed his great love for us by sending Christ to die for us while we were still sinners."

Romans 5:8

Just For Fun

Sometimes friends send me little clippings from newspapers or magazines that brighten my day with their humorous or thoughtful elements. Here are three of my favorites:

From The Associated Press in 1995 with the headline: **Ocean first clue that motorist overshot Arizona.**

"A lost motorist wound up at the end of a freeway next to the Pacific Ocean after he completely missed Arizona while driving from New Mexico.

A tow-truck driver found the motorist sitting in his car alongside Interstate 8 where it stops at Ocean Beach in San Diego. The unidentified motorist had a map in his lap and a perplexed look on his face. The motorist said he had come from New Mexico and was looking for Arizona. He offered no explanation on how he missed the state."

Another favorite is an excerpt from *Reader's Digest*, "Laughter, The Best Medicine." Although I do not want to belittle legitimate psychiatric cases, finding humor in our circumstances is usually helpful.

"Hello, welcome to the Psychiatric Hotline."

"If you are obsessive-compulsive, please press 1 repeatedly."

"If you are co-dependent, please ask someone to press 2."

"If you have multiple personalities, please press 3, 4, 5, and 6."

"If you are paranoid-delusional, we know who you are and what you want; just stay on the line until we can trace the call."

"If you are schizophrenic, listen carefully and a little voice will tell you what to do."

"If you are manic-depressive, it doesn't matter which number you press. No one will answer."

Finally, here is the story from the book, *The Conway Twitty Story*, by Wilbur Cross and Michael Kosser. In this book, Twitty talks about how he used to be jealous of other singers who would get recognized while he remained obscure. His jealousy was cured, however, when he heard the following story:

A missionary who had been in China for many years and a famous entertainer who had been there for two weeks were traveling back to the States on the same boat. When they docked in New York, the missionary saw a crowd of the entertainer's fans waiting at the pier. "Lord, I do not understand," the missionary said. "I gave 42 years of my life to China, and he gave only two weeks, yet there are thousands welcoming him home and nobody here to welcome me."

And the Lord replied, "Son, you are not home yet."

Whether you are feeling totally lost, like the motorist who overshot Arizona; ready to call the psychiatric hotline; or just plain discouraged by comparing yourself with someone else; remember that your real home lies elsewhere. Everything that you can see here on earth will one day disappear. It is important to keep a sense of humor and a perspective about what is really important. Do not let the unimportant things in life discourage you.

"Sell what you have and give to those in need. This will fatten your purses in heaven! And the purses of heaven have no rips or holes in them. Your treasures there will never disappear; no thief can steal them; no moth can destroy them."

Luke 12:33

The Pleasure of Giving

When my daughter, Deanna, was nineteen years old, she met a young man, Mohamadou, from The Gambia, a small country in West Africa. He was attending college with her in the United States and they became very good friends.

Shortly after they met, around Christmas, Deanna found a small box and a card in her student mailbox with Mohamadou's return address. On opening them, she discovered a beautiful Christmas card and an exquisite necklace. It was such a thoughtful and lovely gift that at first she was taken aback. She was not expecting any gift at all, let alone one so beautiful, and she was not sure how to respond. Within moments, she also realized that she did not have a gift to give in return. Feeling embarrassed, Deanna was at a loss as to how to respond or what to say to Mohamadou when she saw him again.

The next day the problem solved itself when she ran into him at the student union building. Before Deanna could say anything, Mohamadou stopped her with this request:

"Do not say a word, please. Just do not say anything. Let me speak first."

With wide-eyes and a nod of agreement, Deanna waited to hear what he had to say next. After a short pause, when he was sure he had her attention, he said,

"It was *my* pleasure."

The directness of his statement silenced her for a moment as she let his meaning penetrate her mind. After a second, she then began to stammer that at least she wanted to say "thank you." Mohamadou just shook his head and surprised her even more by his next comment.

"In my country, everyone, small children to old people, give gifts at Christmas. I have no one to give gifts to here. I know very few people in the United States, and my family is in Africa. You are my friend, and again I say it was *my* pleasure."

Feeling chagrined, Deanna mutely stood there trying to take in all of his words. He then asked her a very thought-provoking question.

"Why is it that American women cannot accept gifts or common courtesy? Please realize that I like being courteous to women, and I give gifts because I *want* to give."

Twenty years have passed since Deanna's encounter with Mohamadou, but she has never forgotten the lesson he taught her. Even now, although he has returned to live in The Gambia, they write to each other and have maintained their friendship.

Deanna often reflects on Mohamadou's gift to her and what she calls "the greater gift within the gift." She does not just remember the card and necklace, but also the greater gift of the exchange of joy that she shared through his friendship and thoughtfulness to her. She learned that there is nothing better than the pleasure of giving a gift to someone and knowing that it has brought them joy. This wonderful exchange of joy, between the giver and the recipient, is often worth more than the actual gift.

So, too, God loves to give good gifts to us. He loves to see our faces light up with delight as we realize that He has been thinking about us enough to give us a gift. More important, though, He wants us to recognize the greater gift within the gift – the exchange of joy – and appreciate Him all the more.

"Those you help will be glad not only because of your generous gifts to themselves and to others, but they will praise God for this proof that your deeds are as good as your doctrine."

II Corinthians 9:13

"Thank God for his Son – his Gift too wonderful for words."

II Corinthians 9:15

God's Grace

Once in awhile, a story comes my way that makes me smile, but also teaches me a great truth. The following is one of those stories and was told to me by my pastor, Dr. John Merritt. Although I know that this illustration is not theologically correct, it makes such a good point that I wanted to share it.

There once was a minister who dreamed that he died and was standing in front of the pearly gates of heaven. St. Peter was at the gate and told the minister that he needed one hundred points in order to get into heaven.

"Well," said the minister proudly, "I was the leader of a great church for forty-seven years."

"One point," said Peter.

"One point? That is all I get for forty-seven years of service?"

"Yes, that is correct," replied Peter.

"Hmmm," said the minister, "Well, I visited shut-ins every week."

"One more point," announced Peter.

"I worked with the youth...and you know what that is like!" said the minister.

"One point," said Peter.

"I developed recovery programs for those in crisis."

"One point," continued Peter, "Now you have four points. You need ninety-six more."

Feeling panic and discouragement, the minister tried to wrack his brain for further evidence of his good works. Nothing significant came to mind. Finally, in despair he cried out, "I am desperate and hopeless! I feel so inadequate. Except for the grace of God, I do not stand a chance."

To which Peter smiled and said, "Grace of God, ninety-six points. Come on in!"

"But when the time came for the kindness and love of God our Savior to appear, then he saved us -- not because we were good enough to be saved, but because of his kindness and pity -- by washing away our sins and giving us the new joy of the indwelling Holy Spirit..."

Titus 3:4-6

He Will Know

During my father's last illness, while he was dying of cancer, his four children were with him day and night. We all had the chance to talk over many issues with Dad and let him know how much we loved him. We even let Dad know that we were releasing him and giving him permission to go home to be with the Lord. We did not want him to linger around in pain any longer than was necessary.

It was my deepest desire to physically be there with Dad when he went home to be with the Lord. I knew that he had a very short time to live and I wanted to stay close to him until the end. I also knew, however, that I could not cancel my scheduled speaking engagements planned for each Friday and Saturday. These conferences are booked months or even years in advance. The publicity and work done by the hosting church is considerable.

On Thursday evening, as I was preparing for my flight the next morning, I was crying and having a very difficult time accepting the fact that I could not stay. My sweet twin sister, Judy, who has such deep spiritual insight, came and started weeping with me. As we held each other and cried, Judy gently said, "It is okay, Joanne. Dad would want you to go, as you will be talking to the women about Jesus. If Dad dies while you are gone speaking, he will know what is happening. He will know about all the women who come to accept Jesus. He will know. He will see the angels rejoicing in heaven and he will be rejoicing with them. Do not worry, Joanne. He will know." Judy's words made my parting from Dad more bearable. She was right; Dad would have wanted me to go.

I went to the conference and spoke about how Jesus died for us so that we can be forgiven of our sins and made whole. Many of the women who attended came to know the Lord for the very first time. I was so excited to rush back to Dad's side and tell him all about it, but I never got the chance. The angels beat me to it. My Dad died that weekend -- but he knew. He knew.

"...A woman has ten valuable silver coins and loses one. Won't she light a lamp and look in every corner of the house and sweep every nook and cranny until she finds it? And then won't she call in her friends and neighbors to rejoice with her? In the same way there is joy in the presence of the angels of God when one sinner repents."

Luke 15:8-10

119

Grandma Does Not Have Enough To Do

When my granddaughter, Fallon, was three and a half years old, she came to visit me for a couple of days. Since it is difficult for me to have all eight grandchildren visit in a big group, I usually try and take them one at a time and spend a couple of days with each of them just doing things they will enjoy. I love this one-on-one time and try to make it extra special. We talk by the hour, play games, go shopping, and watch movies, but most of all we laugh.

After two days of hilarious fun and laughing together, it was time for Fallon to go home. On the day I was to take her home I kept telling her how wonderful she was and how much fun I had had with her. She seemed to drink in all the attention and listened especially well when I said how much I would miss her when she was gone and how I hoped she would come back to visit soon.

Although Fallon is not an overly talkative child, I could tell she was unusually quiet as we made the hour and a half drive back to her house. Her furrowed brow and concentrated expression told me that she was deep in thought about something that was troubling her. It was obvious that she was trying to come up with a solution to a very knotty problem.

With her three year old mind working overtime, suddenly the proverbial light bulb went on and she pronounced her solution to the problem on her mind. With great compassion and earnestness she said, "I wish you had a kid like me!"

What? I thought to myself. *Where did she come up with an idea like that?* Trying to validate her feelings, I smiled and chuckled as I said, "Well, I wish I had a kid like you too!"

Somehow this did not satisfy her and my response only seemed to provoke a more worried look on her face. I gathered that she was trying to figure out how to give me a kid like her. Since I could not understand why she would want to do this, I thought I had better clarify with her just what was on her mind.

"Why do you want Grandma to have a kid like you?" I asked Fallon.

"Because then you would not cry all day and be lonely when I am not there!" she exclaimed with true concern. *Aha! Now I understood. She had translated my missing her into paralyzing grief*

that made it difficult for me to function normally.
What a burden for her!

"Do you think that Grandma cries all day when you are not around?"

"Yes!"

Still chuckling to myself, I gently let her know that as much as I missed her, I did do a few other things during the day! She seemed relieved by this and happy to know that I could plan and do many things in between spending time with her.

As I reflect on this incident, I am reminded of how we sometimes view God as a genie in a lamp, inactive until we rub the lamp and ask for our wishes to be granted. What a poor life God would have if He were just sitting around waiting for us to have time to spend with Him, but of course that is not the reality at all. Yes, He misses us when we are away from Him, but He is not incapacitated during our time away!

We are the ones who miss out when we do not spend time with Him. God has planned many activities for us and wants to shower us with His blessings. I am not sure about you, but I do not want to miss any of those blessings! Like Fallon, I want God to "have a kid like me" around at all times. I know God can function without me, but I do not function well without Him!

"And if you hardhearted, sinful men know how to give good gifts to your children, won't your Father in heaven even more certainly give good gifts to those who ask him for them?"

Matthew 7:11

Learn To Laugh At Yourself!

When I was first learning about God-given confidence, I was working with a woman named Mrs. Dooley.* She was my boss back in 1968 when I first started working at a modeling school in Eugene, Oregon.

Mrs. Dooley was a very prim and proper woman. She acted high and mighty with everyone and generally heaped disdain on those around her who did not reach her own perceived pinnacle of loftiness. Needless to say, she was a very difficult woman, especially when you had to work for her.

Mrs. Dooley, however, is not remembered in our family as a difficult woman. She is not remembered for her great aura of sophistication. Instead, she is remembered as a very silly woman with a very foolish attitude. I get the giggles every

---

* name has been changed

time I think about her, which I am sure would irritate her if she knew.

I cannot help laughing as I remember an incident that occurred when Mrs. Dooley invited me (along with my two children, Deanna and Bobby) to have lunch at the Hilton Hotel's restaurant in Eugene. The Hilton Hotel was the tallest building in town and the restaurant was the ritziest, fanciest restaurant doing business at that time. To be invited there was quite a treat for all of us.

I arrived at the restaurant with my kids, then age nine and seven, in tow. All three of us were dressed up for the occasion. On the way over I had reminded both children several times to be on their best behavior. I explicitly told them to sit properly, act like adults should, and for goodness sakes, not to play around or make any noise!

Mrs. Dooley was waiting for us at a square table in the center of the room. It was conspicuous and it was obviously chosen so that we could all be on display. Mrs. Dooley wanted to make sure everyone would notice her in her Jackie Kennedy pillbox-hat and matching suit finery.

I sat next to Mrs. Dooley on her right with the children seated across from us. Once we had all taken our seats and had ordered, we settled in for a few moments of small talk. In her loftiest voice, Mrs. Dooley said:

"Oh, Joanne, I just *lo-oove* your outfit. Where did you get it?"

"I really cannot remember," I replied meekly.

"Well, let me see if I can find out who designed it," she announced as she leaned over in her chair and reached for the back of my dress where the tags were.

Evidently she was sitting a little further away than she realized, because as she continued to lean over to get a better view of the label, she lost her balance. Her chair began to slide out from under her and then tipped completely over, slid across the room and dumped Mrs. Dooley unceremoniously onto the floor! She landed smack on her side, legs flailing, in view of the whole restaurant! It was an *America's Funniest Home Videos* moment that would have won the $100,000 prize.

I had to bite my lip to keep from laughing as I tried to help Mrs. Dooley get off the floor. Fortunately for her, she was physically unhurt. Unfortunately for me, when I looked up at my kids, they were smirking at me with dancing eyes. I looked back down at Mrs. Dooley in desperation. She was most definitely not laughing. My kids were having trouble controlling their giggles. I wanted to laugh, but I just did not dare.

Mrs. Dooley would not even acknowledge that she had fallen. Her mask of snobbery prevailed, although I am sure she must have been mortified on the inside. It was as if she could not admit the fall even to herself. If only she could have had a sense of humor about it and laughed it off. Instead, she just ended up looking more foolish.

Throughout the rest of the meal, I had to keep kicking my children under the table and giving them stern looks to keep them from laughing. We had to sit through the entire lunch as if nothing had happened. It seemed an eternity before Mrs. Dooley finally excused herself and exited the restaurant. Once she was out the door, we all burst into wild and hilarious laughter. We just could not stop! I thought our sides would burst from laughing so much!

Poor Mrs. Dooley, with all her finery and sophistication still fell flat on her face. To make matters worse, our family has been laughing about her fall ever since!

Falling with grace is an important lesson to learn. It is not the fall that is so important, it is how you pick yourself up and what you learn from it afterwards. I have fallen on my face a few times (both literally and figuratively) and I have learned from Mrs. Dooley's bad example. I hope I will go down in history as a real and honest person, instead of one who hides behind a snob's unflattering mask. I have learned that it is better to laugh at myself before others do -- then simply continue on with life.

"Do not rejoice against me, O my enemy,
for though I fall, I will rise again!
When I sit in darkness,
the Lord himself will be my Light."

Micah 7:8

Speaking The Truth In Love

My granddaughter, Shaina, is a beautiful, dramatic, and enthusiastic young woman. She is full of ideas and loves to talk about whatever comes to mind. She sometimes has trouble thinking before she speaks and this has gotten her into some embarrassing moments.

When she was seven years old, her natural tendency to say the first thing that popped out of her mouth was very apparent. She would tell total strangers that they needed to comb their hair, or clean their clothes, or take care of an acne problem. She even asked a very wrinkled seventy-year-old woman what had happened to her face!

Around this time she came to my house for a visit and was sitting on my lap talking with me. I noticed her looking at the aging fullness of skin under my chin. Touching it she said, "I am never going to get old like you, Grandma. I do not want to have that ugly stuff under my chin!"

I used to despair that Shaina would ever learn tact, but somehow life has a way of teaching us valuable lessons. For Shaina, the day came when she was about eight-years-old.

Important to this story is that Shaina is African-American, but her adoptive parents are both Anglo-American. One day Shaina was standing in line with her dad waiting to order at McDonald's restaurant. An African-American man also waiting in line overheard her calling, "Daddy, Daddy" to her white father. Looking from Shaina to her father and back to Shaina again, you could see that this man's brain was trying to sort out the puzzle.

Finally, with the look of one who has solved a great mystery, the man announced to Shaina, "So...your mother is black!"

To which Shaina quickly retorted, "No, she is white!"

Looking shocked, the man then blurted out, "Well, what happened to *you*?"

Our family laughs a lot about this story. We can appreciate the man's logical dilemma and also how the bluntness of the question let Shaina be on the receiving end of tactless statements. Since that time, Shaina has improved greatly in learning to control her tongue!

Do you have trouble controlling your tongue? Is it hard to remember to *speak the truth* but to speak it *in love?* Hopefully you do not need the kind of reminder that Shaina received.

Before opening your mouth, take the time to consider the impact of your words on the person receiving them. Are you helping to build their self-esteem or self-confidence? Will they be happy that you have spoken to them?

"Let your conversation be gracious
as well as sensible, for then you
will have the right answer
for everyone."

Colossians 4:6

"Everyone enjoys giving good advice,
and how wonderful it is to be
able to say the right thing
at the right time!"

Proverbs 15:23

Another One?

I just sat there in disbelief. Was Deanna crazy? She had just announced to me that she was going to adopt child number seven *as a single parent!* Since Deanna's divorce, I knew that she had had her hands full raising the six children that she already had. What was she thinking?

After thirty-five years of knowing my daughter, I should not have been surprised. Deanna has always "marched to a different drummer," but somehow I was not prepared for the emotions I felt about her decision. The mothering instinct in me wanted to make my daughter's life easier. I wanted to fix everything for her and most of all I wanted her to listen to me and understand that she was making a mistake by taking on another child.

"Deanna," I began, "you have six children already. Isn't that enough for you? How can you afford to take care of another child?"

"Mom," she replied, "people are the only worthwhile investment. Nothing here on earth that we can physically see will make it to heaven with us. Only our relationship with God and others will last. How can I afford *not* to take care of another child? It is what God has called me to do."

That is Deanna for you -- following her heart and trying to listen to God's voice. Well, of course, she was right, much as I did not want to admit it. Silently, I just prayed, *"Lord, help me to accept this situation and not worry about Deanna too much."*

At that moment I had a choice to let go of my expectations for my daughter's life or to hold on and try to run her life for her. Thankfully, the Lord reminded me that I am not responsible for another person's actions, I am only responsible to Him for my own actions. Since Deanna was determined to adopt again, I could either choose to accept it or fight against it (which would cause a horrible rift between us). For my part, I chose to accept it as part of God's plan.

If I had fought against Deanna's decision, I would have missed out on a great joy--my beautiful granddaughter, Tadela. Tadela arrived to the United States from Ethiopia at the age of three and a half years old. She is now seven, and a precious delight to our family. I cannot imagine our family without her and I know that God planned for her to be here all along.

I wish I could say that I learned my lesson once and for all. The truth is that when Deanna announced a couple of years later that she was adopting *another* child (number eight) as a single parent, I again had to go through the process of submitting to God's plan in order to get to the same acceptance level.

My latest grandson, Elijah, also from Ethiopia, is a wonderful addition to our family. I have seen God's plan beautifully unfold.

So far Deanna has not mentioned child number nine!

I am learning to surrender my will to God's will. It is not always an easy process, but one that benefits others and me in the end. Can you say the same thing? Are you learning to bend with God's plans, or are you still trying to bend God's plans to your own?

"O Lord, I know it is not within the power of man to map his life and plan his course -- so you correct me, Lord; but please be gentle..."

Jeremiah 10:23-24

We All Need Each Other

An old rabbi once asked his pupils how they could tell when night had ended and day was on its way back.

"Could it be," asked one student, "when you can see an animal in the distance and tell whether it is a sheep or a dog?"

"No," answered the rabbi.

"Could it be, " asked another student, "when you can look at a tree in the distance and tell whether it is a fig tree or a peach tree?"

"No," answered the rabbi.

His pupils then demanded, "Well, tell us what it is!"

To which the wise old rabbi responded:

"It is when you look on the face of *any* man or woman and see that he or she is your brother or sister. Because if you cannot do this, then no matter what time it is, it is still night."

I believe it is time to drop the barriers of prejudice. God longs to touch other people's lives through you and me. Are we blocking God's plan by refusing to see our brothers and sisters all around us? Is it still "night" where you are living?

Remember that you may have a heart of gold, but so does a hard-boiled egg! It is not enough just to have *good intentions*; instead we must *act* on our beliefs. As Christians, we are all part of God's family. As people, we are all part of the human race. It is time to start seeing others as part of ourselves. We need each other.

*"But whoever loves his fellow man
is 'walking in the light' and
can see his way without stumbling
around in darkness and sin."*

I John 2:10

The Color Green Never Looked So Good

My grandson, Jameson, is one of those rare and gifted individuals who is naturally and genuinely funny. Humorous comments just flow from him. He has always had this gift, starting from the time he could talk.

When Jameson was just two years old, Deanna decided to take all the kids to the zoo. The older children had been talking about it for awhile, but Jameson had never been before and he was really looking forward to seeing all the animals.

It was a two-hour drive to get there, so after loading all the kids in the van and buckling Jameson into his car seat, Deanna headed for the freeway. About fifteen minutes into the trip, she realized she needed some gasoline. As she pulled into the next service station along the route and parked the car at the pump, she noticed Jameson viewing his surroundings with great interest. He looked at the other people filling their cars with gas and got a puzzled expression on his face. You could see by his face that his brain was working, and finally his voice could be heard from the back seat saying, "You call *this* a zoo?"

Another time, when Jameson was about seven years old, I picked him up from his house so he could stay with me for a couple of days. It was about a one and a half-hour drive from his house to mine, so before we started out on the trip we stopped at a mini-mart to buy a big slushy soft drink. Jameson promised me that he could drink the whole thing and still make it home before having to go to the bathroom. He knew that there were very few restrooms off the freeway between his house and mine.

Of course, being a kid, he had to go to the bathroom just a few minutes after we left the mini-mart, but Jameson assured me that he could "hold it." We continued to drive for another hour or so until we finally exited at my hometown. Just a couple of miles down a busy boulevard (with numerous stoplights), and we would be at my house. By this time, Jameson was wiggling and giggling. He also looked tremendously relieved every time we went through an intersection without having to stop for a red light.

The last intersection before my house was just ahead. Poor Jameson watched with a tight grimace on his face as the light turned red before we could get through. It was a busy intersection. We sat and sat for what seemed like hours. Finally, the light changed and Jameson blurted out, "The color green has never looked *so good!*"

To this day, I chuckle when I am waiting for a long period of time at a red light and it finally turns green. I say to myself, "The color green has never looked so good!" It reminds me of how often we, as human beings, are urgently waiting for the "light to turn green."

Do you feel that you have been sitting at the stoplight for too long? All of us can feel impatient, but sometimes it is important to realize that even red lights have their purpose. With God, no time is wasted. We are admonished to make the most of every moment we have to live for Him.

When we are so busy "waiting for the light to turn green," we may miss God's call to wait on *Him.* It is really His plan that we are to follow, not our own. In His timing, waiting may be the best thing for us. Can you sit at the stoplight just a little longer?

"So be careful how you act;
these are difficult days.
Don't be fools; be wise:
make the most
of every opportunity
you have for doing good."

Ephesians 5:15-16

The Hands of Opportunity

It happened when I went to visit my son, Bob, at his home in New York City. I was riding on the subway, going through town and had just taken my seat. Behind me shuffled an old woman who sat down across from me. Her coat was ragged and not nearly heavy enough to protect her from the bitter New York wind. Her shoulders were hunched against the cold and her eyes looked down. I noticed that her hands were very white, cracked, and bony. She clutched a worn, thin shawl tightly around her shoulders. She wore no gloves. I watched her for a moment with great pity.

At the next stop, I noticed an energetic young woman walk confidently onto the train. Her cheeks were red with health. Her hair was shiny and immaculate. Her clothes were beautiful. Her warm leather gloves looked brand new. As she sat down beside me, I noticed that she too watched the old woman with pity.

The train continued on its journey until finally the young woman's destination was reached. As the train slowed to a stop, I saw the young woman glide past the old woman and then disappear out the door and into the tunnel. The train started moving again and I looked at the old woman. There, on her lap, I saw the young woman's new leather gloves.

I will never know if that young woman was a believer in Christ or not. I do know this: she saw a person in need and responded with compassion -- while I just sat there. It hurts to realize that it never occurred to me to give the old woman *my* gloves.

I am humbled whenever I stop to think about that young woman who showed Christ's compassion on a subway train in New York.

"He will take care of the helpless
and poor when they cry to him;
for they have no one else
to defend them.
He feels pity for the weak
and needy, and will rescue them."

Psalm 72:12-13

Rushing To Nowhere

When Deanna was a teenager we used to love to go to the Miss Oregon pageant together. We lived in Oregon then and Deanna had once competed in the pageant, so it was a treat for us to go to Seaside, Oregon (where the pageant is held) and spend the weekend together, just mother and daughter.

This one particular year, when Deanna was nineteen, I was consumed with work and rushing around like crazy to get everything done so we could hop in the car on Friday afternoon and drive two and a half hours to the preliminary pageant that night. I had marked my calendar and put the tickets in my wallet so that I would not forget.

When Deanna arrived home from work I told her to hurry up and grab her suitcase because we needed to get going right away. I also grabbed my bag and practically ran to the car.

Once we were on our way I just could not relax. I have always been one for organization and planning. I do not like to feel rushed or hurried. I sometimes overdo it and I have the tendency to plan everything out and then say, "Lord, are *You* coming?"

So on that day we drove two and a half hours to Seaside. When we got there we noticed that the traffic was very light. I commented that it was unusual to have such little traffic on the weekend of the Miss Oregon pageant. Deanna agreed with me, but then added, "Well, I think we are late, Mom. We had better hurry up. Everyone is probably already there!"

Stepping on the gas, we arrived at the Seaside Convention Center in a matter of minutes. The pageant is always held there, but when we pulled into the parking lot we noticed right away that it was empty! I turned to Deanna and said, "What is going on now?"

As I looked up at the marquee board outside the building, I noticed that it read, *Flea Market This Weekend.* Out loud I said to Deanna, "Flea Market? What in the world?"

"Oh, Mom, I think I know. Possibly the pageant is being held at the high school this year because there were too few contestants. We had better hurry and rush over to the high school right away!"

What Deanna said made sense to me, so I started to pull out of the parking lot. Suddenly, however, a sinking feeling hit my stomach. Putting on the brakes, I said, "Deanna, I have a terrible feeling. I think I had better check our tickets."

Pulling the tickets out of my wallet, I read the dates for the Miss Oregon pageant. Sure enough it said that the pageant was being held the next weekend. The next weekend! How could that be? I am always so organized and prompt. I could never have put the wrong date down on my calendar, could I?

As I told Deanna about the mistake I was feeling upset. Deanna just started to laugh and laugh. She laughed so hard that she had to slap her knee and exclaim, "I love it, I love it, I love it!"

"Deanna, what are you laughing about?"

"I love it, mom! This is the best day of my life! I love it because you cannot do a thing about it!"

I still was not ready to let go of my frustration, but Deanna's laughter started to get through to me. I realized that I was caught in another situation I could not control. What was I going to do about it -- continue to be upset or decide to laugh along with Deanna?

As I was contemplating this, Deanna looked at me with a mischievous grin and said, "Hey, Mom, just think about this. God has been looking down from heaven and watching us as we drove all that way. I can just see Him shaking His head and smiling as He says, 'There they go...on the wrong weekend!'"

At that point, I just started laughing along with Deanna. We both laughed until tears rolled down our cheeks. There we were, all the way in

Seaside on the wrong weekend, but willing to make the best of it. As it turned out, we had the most wonderful time together. We enjoyed the beach, talked, laughed, and even had a pillow fight in the motel room. When we went to the grocery store, we got the giggles and acted very silly. I do not think the grocery store has ever been the same since then!

Deanna and I both learned a valuable lesson that weekend. We got to spend quality time together and built memories that will last a lifetime. In addition, we both found out that it is not enough to just plan for the future. It is more important to make the most of the situation when those plans change.

"Don't brag about your plans for tomorrow--wait and see what happens!"

Proverbs 27:1

Fantastic Feast

Not too long ago I had one of the best experiences when I traveled to South Carolina to speak at a church women's retreat. The senior pastor of the church, Todd Brady, and his wife, Angela, welcomed me into their home like family. Not only was I treated with love, but also for the first time in over thirty years of speaking, the pastor of the church personally cooked dinner for me.

This dinner was no ordinary affair. It was a food lover's paradise! The menu included Cajun fried turkey, pecan-sweet potato souffle, cheddar cheese and broccoli casserole, fresh summer vegetables sauteed in olive oil and spices: yellow squash, zucchini, vidalia onions, sweet creamed corn, hot yeast rolls, and for dessert there was homemade cherry cheesecake and raisin walnut carrot cake.

When I think about the love that went into making such a scrumptious feast, I cannot help but think about Christ's love to all of us and the fact that He is really our spiritual food.

We can eat all the good food provided to us on earth (and Pastor Brady's feast was *greatly* appreciated), but that is not where our focus should be. Instead, we should seek after the eternal food Christ offers to us.

It reminds me of the Bible passage in John 6 after Jesus miraculously fed the multitude with only two fishes and five loaves of bread. The very next day he talked to the crowd that gathered to follow Him and said, "The truth of the matter is that you want to be with me because I fed you, not because you believe in me." (John 6:26)

Defensively, the crowd answered back; "...You must show us more miracles if you want us to believe you are the Messiah. Give us free bread every day..." (John 6: 30)

To which Jesus replied, "I am the Bread of Life. No one coming to me will ever be hungry again. Those believing in me will never thirst." (John 6:35)

Here on this earth, after eating a wonderful feast, I am usually stuffed full. The next day, however, I am hungry again (sometimes even later the same day). As human beings, no matter how much we fill our stomachs with food, eventually if enough time goes by, we will become hungry again.

Spiritually, however, Christ offers us complete satisfaction so that we will never be hungry or thirsty again. He is the source of all our daily spiritual requirements to maintain a healthy life. Now that is what I call a fantastic feast!

"I am the true Bread from heaven; and anyone who eats this Bread shall live forever..."

John 6:58

Letting The Walls Come Down

I recently received the following letter from one of the women who heard me speak at her church's retreat. Her story is heartbreaking, but ultimately inspiring. Here is what she wrote:

Dear Joanne,

I wanted to first of all thank you for coming and speaking at our retreat.

I am always amazed at the many different ways God uses us when we are not even aware of it. Very often it is the tragic things in our lives that God uses to give us a better understanding in helping others in similar situations. I am sorry for all the things you have had to go through, and I am really thankful that you did not give up and you have allowed God to use your past and make you more sensitive to others by offering them hope and encouragement.

I am thirty-six years old. I love the Lord and love serving Him. I am the lady who is stretched in fifty different directions all helping others. I am always smiling and always doing good deeds and saying I am fine. Inside I am bleeding. I see myself cut and sliced up and the pain is incredible.

Nineteen years ago I gave birth to a daughter. She was born to me after I was raped, but she was mine and I loved her. When she was six months old, she was taken from me and killed. You cannot imagine the depth of the hatred I have for myself because I could not save her. I was her mother; I should have protected her.

There is so much pain and guilt and anger for failing her. I have gone through periods of anorexia and bulimia. When the pain started getting worse (eight years ago), I began taking razor blades and cutting myself, thinking all the while that I deserved this and much more. I felt that nothing I could do to hurt myself would ever be punishment enough.

About four years ago I hit bottom. The pain was so overwhelming I could not stand it. I remember going into my bathroom and taking a razor and cutting my wrist twice. I watched the blood run into the sink and this time it was not taking the pain away. I remember grabbing the razor again and I started cutting again, but this time I was determined to cut my hand off. I thought that then the pain would finally go away and maybe that would be punishment enough for not protecting my daughter.

As I started to make that third cut, my husband opened the bathroom door and found me.

He got the razor from me and rushed me to the hospital. But, that was not the end. On the way there I took half a bottle of prescription sleeping pills. I wanted to die.

When I got to the hospital, one of the nurses said to me, "You must be in a lot of pain to do this to yourself." That was the first time anyone had ever acknowledged that I might have pain.

I made it through that time, but I never told anyone what my pain was about. I have kept it a secret and still do.

Over the past four years I have heard God say to me, "I love you. Please let me love you. Do not blame yourself for your daughter's death. It was not your fault. You do not have to keep hurting yourself. You need to forgive yourself."

I just could not believe that I deserved God's love. I kept pushing Him away, until this past weekend when I heard you speaking about your own pain.

At the retreat, as you walked us through the forgiveness prayer, I was finally able to forgive myself. When I walked through that prayer, I saw Jesus in my head and He was wearing a soft white gown. I was kneeling with my head in His lap. I felt like I was 17 again. In my mind's eye, Jesus was stroking my hair and telling me He knew everything and it was okay -- I am okay -- and that I had to forgive myself.

Now the wall of pain is gone. For the first time I do not feel like I have to cut myself or hurt myself. I do not have to punish myself anymore.

I am glad that you were willing to come to our retreat. I know that God has used you to help me to hold on. Because of your willingness to share the pain in your own life, God has used it to help give me a new life. Thank you.

After reading this woman's letter, I could only breathe a prayer of thanks to the Lord. It was only through His grace that she could be healed.

Later, however, I started thinking. How many times do I feel overwhelmed or worthless, consumed by my own pain? What if I more often remembered that by sharing my pain and ultimate healing, others could be set free? I think it would be wonderful to see all those walls of pain come down.

By extension, it's not just me whose pain can be used by God to help bring new life. The whole point of Christ's death on the cross is that He took my pain -- and yours too -- on Himself so that we could be healed.

Are you willing to stop holding onto your pain? Can you accept His healing and let Him use your pain for His glory?

"Yet it was _our_ grief he bore, _our_ sorrows that weighed him down...But he was wounded and bruised for _our_ sins. He was chastised that we might have peace; he was lashed --- and we were healed."

Isaiah 53: 4-5

Unusual Roads

My grandson, Elijah, was adopted from Ethiopia and came to the United States when he was ten years old. A couple of years before his arrival in this country, he was walking down a road in Ethiopia and came alongside a truck being loaded with heavy crates. At that moment, the crane being used to lift the cargo suddenly lost its load and before he could move out of the way, the crates crashed down on Elijah.

The force of the impact threw Elijah face down onto the ground while the cargo landed on his back and legs. Both of his legs were broken and the left leg suffered a compound fracture where the broken bone punctured the skin.

Unable to afford medical treatment, Elijah's birth father took his severely wounded son home. At home, Elijah's stepmother (his birth mother had died two years before) and his two younger sisters tried to take care of him. Unfortunately, within a few days the left leg became infected with gangrene. On the tenth day after the accident,

Elijah was near death and his father took him to a hospital several hours away in Addis Ababa, the capital city of Ethiopia.

Upon arriving at the hospital, the doctors immediately made the decision to amputate Elijah's infected leg. It was an excruciating decision, but ultimately the only one that would save his life. Even after the amputation, Elijah was still not out of danger and the next two weeks were critical for his survival. As the doctors worked to save Elijah's life, Elijah's father worried about how he would pay for the medical costs and also take care of Elijah after his recovery. With scant resources to feed his family, and little hope for disabled people in Ethiopia, Elijah's father was faced with the knowledge of a bleak future for his son. Knowing that Elijah could only be helped by continuing to stay at the hospital with trained medical personnel and the possibility of further assistance, his father made a heartrending decision: he abandoned Elijah at the hospital and never came back.

For the next one and a half years, Elijah lived at the Black Lion Hospital in Addis Ababa. He slowly regained his health and even started to attend school for the first time. Although he never saw his birth family again, he became close to some of the hospital workers and they loved and cared for him along with some of the other children who had been similarly abandoned there.

During this time, Deanna was working with an adoption agency helping to find homes for Ethiopian children. One day at work, a small packet arrived on her desk. Inside the packet were photographs of Ethiopian children needing homes, including two photographs of Elijah. With just one look at Elijah's photographs, Deanna immediately fell in love with his beautiful face, intelligent eyes, and courageous smile. In that instant, God spoke to her heart. Out loud she said to her coworker, "This one is mine."

If you know Deanna, you know that those words were not spoken lightly. A few months later, she flew to Ethiopia to bring Elijah home as her new son and eighth child.

At the time of Elijah's abandonment in the hospital, I am sure there was no way he could have foreseen that his life would someday have joy again. It probably never occurred to him that his life could take such unusual roads and eventually lead him all the way to the other side of the world to a new family.

Elijah may not have foreseen his future, but God did. In God's far-reaching plans, even the worst of circumstances can be transformed into joy.

When I look at Elijah now, with his smiling eyes as he walks around with his new prosthetic leg, I cannot help but be reminded of the story of Joseph in the Bible. Joseph's brothers sold him into slavery and meant to cause him great harm. God, however, had another plan in mind and used Joseph's tragic circumstances to bring about great good for both Joseph and his family. (You can read the story in Genesis 37 & 39-45.)

Thinking about Joseph and my grandson, Elijah, I am reminded that God can transform my own difficult circumstances in mighty ways. It encourages me that God can take such seemingly tragic events and still make something beautiful out of them.

Are you struggling with your own version of tragic circumstances? Does it seem to you that God will never be able to make anything new or wonderful out of them? Take hope into your heart when you consider Elijah's story. Take hope into your life when you consider Joseph's story. Take hope into your personal circumstances as you consider your own story. Understand that God can transform tragedy into great joy.

*"And we know that all that happens
to us is working for our good
if we love God
and are fitting into his plans."*

Romans 8:28

Wait Before The Lord

Our fast-paced culture has drowned out silence. What we hear on television:

Go
Act now
Don't wait
Hurry

What we *never* hear on television:

Stop
Be quiet
Wait awhile
Contemplate a little

With the preponderance of messages telling us that we must move quickly, it is no wonder we have lost the art of listening in silence and waiting patiently. We have become people who get irritated waiting for a fax, think overnight delivery is too slow, and gulp down remedies for "fast, fast, relief."

Recently, Deanna and I spent a few days at the beach together (just the two of us with no children). By the second day, Deanna softly said to me, "Mom, I do not know what to do with all this quiet!"

Someone wisely said, "We must go slowly, because we have no time to waste." Did you catch that? Stop for a minute and think about it: *We must go slowly because we have no time to waste.*

Many of us are wasting our lives by going non-stop. We believe that success comes by *doing.* We have grown up hearing the words, "Don't just *stand* there. Do something!"

What if the opposite is true? What do you suppose God would say? To my heart's ear I think He would say, "Don't just do something. Stand there."

Can you hear Him say those words to you? If you are like most of us, it is difficult to hold still long enough to listen to God. Most of us need to learn how to be still. We need to learn to wait. It is time to stop and wait for God to speak to us.

We must go slowly because we have no time to waste.

"For since the world began no one has seen or heard of such a God as ours, who works for those who wait for him!"

Isaiah 64:4
157

Lullaby Blues

Deanna has a friend, Jane, a single mom of three daughters with special needs. Jane's oldest is Shannon, age twelve, who is moderately autistic with Tourette's Syndrome (a neurological disorder characterized by tics -- rapid, sudden movements or vocalizations that occur repeatedly in the same way). Her middle daughter, Shivonne, is seven, and has Bipolar Disorder (also known as manic-depressive illness characterized by mood swings from extreme highs to extreme lows) and Attention-Deficit Hyperactivity Disorder. Shinae, age five, has Pervasive Developmental Disorder (autism and other disorders) and hypotonia (floppy, decreased muscle tone). Of the three girls, Shivonne, the middle child, is the closest to "normal."

For Jane, the work and emotional load of taking care of her daughters plus holding down a full-time job is considerable. Autistic children often live in their own world and do not usually relate well with others. It is rare for them to have a sense of empathy for someone else. Although Jane pours herself out to care for her children, she is rarely rewarded with a sense of appreciation. She is able to manage with God's grace and has learned to emphasize the small and tender moments she does share with her children. Here is Jane's account of a recent bittersweet incident:

When I tuck the girls into bed, we always pray and listen to a beautiful lullaby recording. Shannon (age twelve) sleeps in a room by herself and Shivonne (age seven) and Shinae (age five) share a room. I usually stay with the younger girls until they fall asleep.

One night, with the music softly playing in the background, I heard Shivonne's little voice say to me, "Mommy, something is breaking my heart."

I, of course, asked her what she meant.

"Well, the kids on the bus make fun of me. They call me fat and stupid and weird. That breaks my heart."

I told her that when I was little the other kids did the same thing to me and it hurt so much. I told her that we had to remember that some people are mean and say things that are not true. I told her that I loved her and many people loved her -- that she was beautiful and smart. We prayed that she would feel better and that the other kids would stop picking on her.

I really did not know what else to say. I got tears in my eyes because I remembered how horrible it felt to have it done to me as a child. I wished that no one would ever do that to my daughter.

As I again sat in the dark, listening to the music, I heard Shivonne's voice once more.

"Mommy, something else is breaking my heart."

Again I asked her what she meant.

"Mommy, it breaks my heart that my sisters are not more like me. I love them so much. The kids on the bus call them weird and make fun of them."

I tried to answer, but I just could not. I started to cry quietly, but of course Shivonne and Shinae could still tell that I was crying.

In that moment, from the other side of the room, my five-year-old, Shinae, softly said,

"Mommy, don't cry. It's okay."

For Jane, Shinae's words of comfort were a very special gift. For a brief moment in time, Shinae was able to reach outside herself to try and understand her mother's pain. It is those types of moments that make it possible for Jane to keep going.

I often think about how many of us may need just one small moment of empathy and how God is always ready to provide it. He is the great lover of our soul, and He knows us inside out. We can have the great assurance that He empathizes with us like no one else can. If you are hurt, lost, or alone, just tell Him about it. He will understand and give you the comfort you need.

*"Sing for joy, O heavens;
shout, O earth.
Break forth with song, O mountains,
for the Lord has comforted his people,
and will have compassion
upon them in their sorrow."*

Isaiah 49:13

Knowing Him

My husband and I were blessed and privileged to be able to take a tour of the Holy Land in Israel. For me, it was the best and most meaningful trip of my life. I walked where Jesus walked. I climbed to the top of the Mount of Olives, which looked down over the Kidron Valley, and I saw the walls of Jerusalem.

Spending time in Israel was such a reverent, humbling, and awe-inspiring event and it was made even more special by the wonderful man who was our tour guide. I really believe he was one of the best tour guides in Israel. He was extremely wise, witty, and personable, and soon won the hearts of all the people on our tour.

Each day he greeted us with his winning smile, clever sense of humor, and incredible knowledge of the Bible. He knew everything from Genesis to Revelation. He knew so much about the Bible that people started to ask, "Is he a believer in Jesus?"

Sadly, the answer was "no."

Our tour guide knew the Bible better than most Christians. He could quote chapter and verse from Jesus' life, but he did not know his own Messiah.

Could that be your situation? Could you have knowledge of God and His son, Jesus, in your head but not your heart? The truth is that knowing *about* Jesus is not the same as actually *knowing Him.*

I believe that it is time for us to really *know* our Savior, Jesus Christ. It is not enough to just be able to quote the Bible. We cannot just intellectualize our relationship with Him. We need to fellowship with Him and really know His heart.

Did you know that He longs to spend time with you today? He longs to share His heart with you. He is just waiting for you to accept Him and have time for Him.

"Look! I have been standing at the door and I am constantly knocking. If anyone hears me calling him and opens the door, I will come in and fellowship with him and he with me."

Revelation 3:20

It Only Takes A Moment

One day I was having lunch with one of my prayer partners, Laura Lou Tolles. We were at a nice, cozy restaurant sitting in a small cubicle in the back so that we actually had a lot of privacy. Our waiter that day was a young man, age twenty-two, who was very talkative and friendly. He noticed that Laura Lou was holding a copy of one of my books, *Mini-Memories For Image Bearers*, which had just been published. I had brought it to share with Laura Lou and it happened to have my photograph on the cover. Looking at the book cover and then up at me, the waiter started to get very excited.

"Hey, wow," he said, "that is you on the front cover! I have a celebrity at my table!"

"No, I am not a celebrity," I answered, "just an ordinary person that happens to have written a book."

"What is the book about?"

"It is mainly about a person's relationship with God," I answered.

"Well," he said, "I had twelve years of theology when I went to a parochial school up the street. Now I am getting my master's degree in psychology."

I wished him well with his studies, but Laura Lou looked at him with a keen expression on her face. With great gentleness, she then spoke to him and said, "Can you say that you have ever received Jesus Christ into your life as your Lord and Savior?"

Thoughtfully he said, "No..."

"That," said Laura Lou, "is what is most important in your life -- that you someday come to a time when you accept Jesus Christ into your life."

"Well," he responded quickly, "how do I do that?"

"Here," replied Laura Lou, "sit right down in this booth beside me and I will show you."

The young man sat down and accepted Christ into his life right there in the restaurant! Guided by Laura Lou, he prayed a very sincere prayer of conversion. After he was finished he said, "You might think this sounds crazy, but I feel different inside now."

Laura Lou and I told him that he had now received the power of God through the Holy Spirit, which was why he felt differently. We invited him to attend church and assured him that we would send him a Bible and other materials.

It was an awesome experience for me! I was inspired and humbled by Laura Lou's quick assessment of the situation with this young man. It made me wonder how many times I have missed opportunities to witness for Christ because I was not sensitive or assertive enough.

So often people are just waiting for us to reach out to them. Remember, it only takes a moment.

"For God loved the world so much that he gave his only Son so that anyone who believes in him shall not perish but have eternal life."

John 3:16

How To Find New Life In Christ

This is what the Bible tells us:

⚹ Your heart tends to run away from God and rebel against Him. The Bible calls this "sin." Romans 3:23 says, "Yes, all have sinned; all fall short of God's glorious ideal."

⚹ Yet God loves you and wants to save you from sin, to offer you a new life of hope. John 10:10 says, "...My purpose is to give life in all its fullness."

⚹ To give you this gift of salvation, God made a way through His Son, Jesus Christ. Romans 5:8 says, "But God showed his great love for us by sending Christ to die for us while we were still sinners."

⁑ You receive this gift by faith alone. Ephesians 2:8 says, "Because of his kindness you have been saved through trusting Christ. And even trusting is not of yourselves; it too is a gift from God."

⁑ Faith is a decision of your heart demonstrated by the actions of your life. Romans 10:9 says, "For if you tell others with your own mouth that Jesus Christ is your Lord, and believe in your own heart that God has raised him from the dead, you will be saved."

⁑ If you are choosing right now to believe Jesus died for your sins and to receive new life through Him, pray a prayer similar to this to thank Him for your new life:

Dear God, I know I am a sinner. I believe Jesus died to forgive me of my sins. I now accept Your offer of eternal life. Thank you for forgiving me of all my sin. Thank You for my new life. From this day forward, I will choose to follow You.

If this expresses the prayer of your heart, I would love to hear from you. Please write to me so that I can encourage you in your new faith.

Order Form

For more information about having Joanne Wallace speak for your church or organization, please fill out the following information:

☐ Yes! Send me information about the possibility of Joanne Wallace speaking in my area.

☐ Rush to me an order form explaining Joanne Wallace's books, audio, and video programs.

My name is: _____

Church/Organization: _____

My address: _____

City: _____ State: _____

Zip Code: _____

Day Phone: _____

Evening Phone: _____

Mail to:

Joanne Wallace

P.O. Box 381

Washougal, WA 98671-0381

Email: joannewallace@mail.com

Web site: www.joannewallace.com

Notes